Come to the House of the Lord

Cover photo:

The Washington, D.C. Temple

by

Mark Poetker, Rockville, Maryland

Come to the House of the Lord

David S. King

Third Printing February 2007

ISBN 13: 978-0-88290-687-4

Published by Horizon Publishers, an imprint of
Cedar Fort, Inc., 2373 West 700 South, Springville, UT, 84663
Distributed by Cedar Fort, Inc., www.cedarfort.com

Printed in the United States of America

10 9 8 7 6 5 4

Printed on acid-free paper

Contents

The Angel Moroni, Ready to be Lifted into Place for the Washington D. C. Temple (Summer, 1974).

Witnesses are, left to right: Elders Thomas S. Monson and Boyd K. Packer, sculptor Avard Fairbanks, author and Bishop David S. King, and Stake President J. Willard Marriott, Sr.

1
Beginnings

Into every lifetime there comes a memorable experience that overshadows all the rest. Mine began with a long-distance call from President Gordon B. Hinckley. In his friendly way he asked me whether I would accept the calling of President of the Washington D. C. temple, and my wife Rosalie, that of matron. An unexpected thunderbolt could not have caught me more by surprise. Rosalie and I had just returned to our home in Kensington, Maryland, after presiding for three years over the Haiti-Port-au-Prince Mission. We already had made other plans, but in the brief moment I had to collect my thoughts, I pushed those plans aside, and accepted what I knew was a calling from the Lord. I was certain that Rosalie would agree.

"It will require a lot of fasting and prayer," I found myself saying. That wasn't exactly an answer to President Hinckley's question, but in my confusion I knew I was on safe ground, and since my head was spinning so fast, I couldn't think of anything else to say. President Hinckley, however, didn't need a more elaborate answer. He correctly concluded that I was saying yes, and after graciously thanking me for accepting the call, proceeded to give me the details.

That little episode marked the beginning of our three-years' experience presiding over one of the Church's three largest temples. The richness of that experience made it the spiritual capstone and the most rewarding event of our lives.

I had always been attracted to the temple, having previously served as patron, ordinance worker, and sealer. In those capacities, I had learned that in today's temples, as in those of old, God and man could meet and enter into a binding covenant that would shape the course of events throughout eternity. No one, having had that awesome experience, could ever be the same again. The experience had also given me the inexpressible joy of becoming a Savior on Mount Zion for those who had gone before me.

The Washington D.C. Temple

After assuming responsibilities as president of the Washington D. C. Temple, located in Kensington, Maryland, I found the history of its origins particularly faith-promoting. I already knew as much about that history as was knowable from just watching the building being constructed, as a bystander. I had served as bishop of the Kensington Ward during that entire period. But when, as temple president, I later discovered some of that history's more intriguing but less-known vignettes, I thought them too good to keep to myself. They strongly confirmed my conviction that God really does "move in a mysterious way, his wonders to perform." Silently and mysteriously, I felt his loving hand guiding the work of the Kingdom as it moved forward to the fulfillment of its destiny.

In order to avoid the appearance of partiality, I freely acknowledge that all of our temples have their own faith-promoting stories to tell. In many of them, beginning with the one in Kirtland, a distinctive leitmotif runs throughout, namely, the struggle of the powers of darkness to delay or thwart the temple's construction, and the countervailing efforts of the forces of light to make it come to fruition.

The history of the Washington D. C. temple is typical of the above, and by relating it I realize that I am doing no more than telling the story of the invincibility of God's design that all his children should eventually enjoy the blessing of a temple.

The Washington D. C. temple is an architectural jewel. As originally envisioned by President David O. McKay, it would face east, as do most of our temples (see Matt. 24:27), and would be dressed in a smooth, windowless, fluted veneer of gleaming white marble, causing the viewer's gaze to involuntarily move upward until it reached the temple's crowning architectural feature, the 14-foot gold-covered statue of the Angel Moroni. The whole concept was dazzling.

During the late 1960's, while the decision was still being pondered in Salt Lake City as to whether the Church should even build a temple in the Washington area, the latter was being convulsed by a series of ugly riots. These occurred ten years before the watershed decision by the Church in 1978, allowing temple access to all worthy members regardless of ethnic origin. There was concern in Salt Lake City, therefore, several years prior to that crucial decision, lest a church building of high visibility might act as a lightning rod to attract hostile demonstrations. This was a real obstacle, and the entire project might have died, right there.

So, at the very threshold, these concerns had to be assuaged, which they finally were, thanks to the efforts of those who could more clearly see the enormous good that a world-class temple could do in our nation's capital. Although these concerns seemed very reasonable at the time, subsequent history has shown that, with one or two very minor exceptions, none of them has ever materialized.

After the project's final approval in principle, in 1968, the next two specific orders of business on the temple agenda were obtaining title to the property which the Church had its eye on, and the acquisition of legal permission to build—two formidable obstacles. What made the acquisition of title to that particular piece of property so critical was that it was the only one in the entire Washington area, and even beyond, that satisfied the conditions that the Church felt should be met before it could give approval. There was literally no other plot anywhere that would do, and for that reason the entire temple project, once again, hung precariously in the balance.

These conditions were that the land had to be: (a) located in the general northwest Washington area; (b) sufficiently large to accommodate a world-class temple and its extensive grounds, gardens, and appurtenances; (c) easily accessible to the general public; (d) sufficiently elevated to make the temple's appearance both visible and majestic; (e) located in a refined and dignified neighborhood; and (f) hopefully wooded, and conducive to a feeling of tranquility and appreciation for the beauties of nature. These were difficult conditions to meet, but providentially the proposed property met all of them. It was the only one that did, and none of the others under consideration came even close. Failure to acquire title to this particular one would have meant a major setback, or even abandonment, of the project.

The Church was encouraged however, in the pursuit of its "project-temple," by the fact that for some reason this particular property had remained vacant for well over three centuries, as though God had been keeping it unspoiled until the time came for its destined use. Those who have traced its legal title from the time of its original British owner, Lord Calvert, to the present, are amazed that it could have remained in its virgin wooded state throughout that entire period, whereas all the surrounding suitable properties for miles around have long since been turned over to private hands for residential and commercial development.

But very tough legal obstacles yet remained. It so happened that in 1968, title to the coveted real estate was vested in a certain group, three of whose principal owners had been authorized by the others to proceed to negotiate for the property's sale. Accordingly, they had already entered into negotiations with a real estate developer who was seriously interested in obtaining the property for private dwelling development. It was precisely at that same time that the Church gave its official approval for the temple project to be put into motion, and authorized Bishop Robert W. Barker, a prominent Latter-day Saint attorney, to do what he could to obtain title to the real estate for the Church.

However, when Bishop Barker contacted the above-mentioned gentlemen representing the owners, he found that negotiations had proceeded to such an extent with the real estate developer that the owners were no longer interested in discussing other offers. Under the circumstances, Bishop Barker, realizing that the situation was desperate, and that the very fate of the entire project was hanging in the balance, felt inspired to lay his cards on the table. In one last attempt to persuade the offerees to accept his offer, he told them that he represented The Church of Jesus Christ of Latter-day Saints. He knew that the three gentlemen were Jewish, and for that reason felt constrained to tell them that the property was to be used for constructing thereon a magnificent temple to Almighty God. He reminded them of the glorious temple-building tradition among the Jewish people, and assured them that the ceremonies in the Latter-day Saint temple would be comparable in significant ways to the ceremonies with which the Jewish people were familiar. He added that the proposed temple would be beautiful, as well as a real credit, both to the city of Washington, and to the entire nation.

Then came the miracle. These three gentlemen did an about-face and accepted, on behalf of the owners, Bishop Barker's offer on behalf of the Church.

Twenty-five years later, Sister Diane L. Holling, a most faithful member of the Church, an architect in her own right, and a devoted patron of the temple, did considerable research on the temple's history in preparation for a book to be written on the Washington Temple. In that connection, she personally interviewed the two survivors of the three original owners of the property in question. One of them was then 97 years old. Both of them agreed that, (a) if Brother Barker's final appeal had come to them *three days later,* it would have been too late, for title to the property by then would have passed to the real estate developer; and (b) in the light of subsequent developments, they were pleased that they had responded the way they did. Sister Holling's careful research resulted in our now having this valuable historical material dealing with the acquisition of the temple property.

Taking advantage of that tiny keyhole of time, the Church was able to acquire a very unusual 57-acre tract of beautifully wooded land upon which to build a temple to the Lord and, later, a visitors' center and chapel. The ground rises 90 feet above a well-traveled beltway, giving the temple a pedestal to make it more visible to the tens of thousands of daily commuters whose attention is unavoidably attracted to its majestic and ethereal appearance.

A number of recent converts to the Church have told us that their interest in their newly acquired faith had first been kindled by the favorable impression of the temple which they had received every day while on their way to work.

The temple and its grounds eventually offered not only a sanctuary for countless temple workers and patrons, but also a Mecca and haven for tens of thousands of tourists and solitary pilgrims. Many of the latter turned to the temple to learn more about the Church or to merely meditate upon the beauties and mysteries of life.

Returning to the 1968 threshold events in the history of the temple's construction, we find evidence that once again miraculous interventions made possible its realization. Although concerned neighbors had repeatedly objected to several previous construction proposals submitted by various developers, their reaction to the Church proposal to build a heroic-size temple in their midst was very positive and without serious objections. As for obtaining approval from the Montgomery County Planning Commission, although a number of very reasonable conditions were imposed, the final permission to build was given with remarkable dispatch.

Today the neighbors of the area are among the temple's most loyal supporters. The sheer splendor of the building itself, surrounded by its incomparable gardens and wooded areas, and bathed in a sweet ambiance of dignity, peace, and tranquility, have enhanced the value of the area for residential purposes and have brought the Church incalculable good will.

Thus, one by one the obstacles were surmounted and the hand of the Lord was felt in the accomplishment of his purposes. The stories of the temple's construction and of the individual sacrifices made by both the poor and the affluent to make that construction possible would fill a volume. Construction was completed in the incredibly short period of thirty-three months and was miraculously accomplished without work stoppages, deaths, or serious injuries.

The agent-contractor, Brother Sid Foulger, with a distinguished career of Church service, later testified that the temple's foundation had been laid sufficiently solidly to enable the building to "last throughout the millennium." It was three times more solid and durable than what was required by the County building code. At the time of his dedicatory prayer in November 1974, President Spencer W. Kimball declared, among other things, that the selection of the temple site and builders had been inspired by the Lord.

Writing This Book

I now return to my experiences as temple president. One of them involved giving a series of lectures to a High Priests group on the history and functions of temples and on my views and personal feelings about them. In delivering these lectures, I was aware that many patrons were not getting the most out of their temple experience, and that I might be able to help them a little by sharing some of my experiences. Many inexperienced patrons, in particular, asked a number of questions revealing a lack of basic understanding of the importance of these temple ordinances. They seemed particularly confused by the numerous symbols, which were unlike anything they had ever experienced.

Moreover, many of the experienced workers also told me that the ordinances had lost some of their original luster and expressed the hope that it might be recaptured by a review of the temple fundamentals which had grown a little hazy in their minds.

The countless resulting questions needed a response. I had to remind my interrogators, however, that there was no way I or anyone else could answer all their inquiries, for there were many aspects of the ordinances that no one was permitted to discuss, even within the temple. I told them that each patron was invited to interpret the temple-text for himself, without coaching. Nevertheless, I did feel that some response could be given that might revitalize a patron's temple experience without betraying any confidences. In some cases I felt that the patron had been inadequately prepared for his temple experience, although with the Church's current emphasis on Temple Preparation classes, examples of this were becoming rarer. I was later encouraged to publish my discussions in the hope that they might reach a larger audience.

Several excellent and scholarly books have already been written on the history and function of temples, and I can add nothing particularly new to the abundance of literature extant. Elder Boyd K Packer's book *The Holy Temple* (Bookcraft, 1980), is basic reading for those who wish to broaden their understanding of the temple from the point of view of a member of the Quorum of the Twelve. The value of my contribution will lie, perhaps, in the thought I have given to some of the questions most frequently asked. My intended beneficiaries are not only those who contemplate visiting the temple for the first time, but also those who frequent the temple but who are hungry still for further insights to make their experience more meaningful. Above all else, I hope to communicate to all faithful Latter-day Saints the sheer joy and excitement which I feel in entering the House of the Lord to perform the ordinances of exaltation for the benefit of those who await their day of deliverance.

One can never fully understand the leaves of a tree without also understanding its roots and the soil in which they grew. A presentation of the temple's historical roots provides me with a framework to which I can affix my own comments and explanatory material. An increased knowledge and understanding will strengthen the temple worker's motivation to continue performing this redemptive work. In this way, I hope to fuel the fires of enthusiasm for all those who take this glorious work seriously.

The Rule of Confidentiality and Non-disclosure

To those who came to my office seeking answers to their questions about the temple ordinances, I had three stock answers.

First, the Church has no official interpretation of any of the temple ordinances, except that contained within the ordinances themselves, or those given in the scriptures. The material found in Doctrine and Covenants 128:12-13 is a good example of the latter. There, the symbolism of baptism for the dead is fully explained. Also, the General Authorities have occasionally made statements of a general nature which throw light on the meaning of the ordinances. For example, they have frequently affirmed that all the temple ordinances are intended to bring us closer to our Savior and to an understanding of his great creative and redemptive roles.

The well-known statement of President Brigham Young regarding the endowment is as follows: "Your endowment is, to receive all those ordinances in the House of the Lord, which are necessary for you, after you have departed this life, to enable you to walk back to the presence of the Father, passing the angels who stand as sentinels, being enabled to give them the key words, the signs and tokens, pertaining to the Holy Priesthood, and gain your eternal exaltation in spite of earth and hell."[1]

The reason for the Church's refusal to go beyond the scriptures and the few statements of the General Authorities in interpreting the temple ceremony for us is that each of us is entitled to a personal revelation from God, bringing as much of its meaning to us as God intends for us to receive. What knowledge we do receive, therefore, must result from our own spiritual exertion. The Church will not interfere with that sacred process. In other words, the Church does not wish to stand between the participant and his Heavenly Father whom he has supplicated for knowledge. If it does, it would be doing for him what he must do for himself (see 2 Ne. 25:23).

Each individual can do a great deal through his own efforts to enlarge his understanding through prayer, meditation, and studying the materials that are available to him, scriptural and otherwise. Noninterference by the Church in this sacred process is based on a wise policy and is consistent with its overall view that each child of God is entitled to his own revelation on matters which concern him personally (see D&C 6:5-7, 15; 9:8; 46:28; Matt.7:7-8).

Moreover, let us not overlook the fact that the temple ceremony is, in all respects that concern us at this time, self-explanatory. Those portions of it which the patron must understand, *he can understand.* There is no ambiguity whatsoever. Beyond that, each participant must pray to God for such further enlightenment as the latter may choose to vouchsafe unto him.

To the spiritually somnolent, the answers to the mysteries of godliness will be slow in coming. Although temple goers are fond of saying that "Every time one enters the temple he learns something new," I suggest that we add to that: "provided he is alert, observant, and spiritually inquisitive."

My second stock answer is that even if the Church did have a full set of explanations for every aspect of the temple ordinances, the temple president's lips would *still* remain sealed. The rule of confidentiality forbids all who have received confidential knowledge of the temple ordinances from divulging or discussing that knowledge with others either *inside* or *outside* the temple. Those who are in training, or who are actually administering the ordinances, are permitted to discuss them inside the temple, of course, but only to the extent necessary to perform their duties.

This exclusionary rule should come as no surprise. Throughout all dispensations of time the Lord has imposed a rule of confidentiality on his children regarding certain sacred matters (see for example, Moses 1:42; 4:32; Matt. 17:9; John 16:12; 3 Ne. 28:14; and D&C 76:114-116).

Though there are many reasons for this, I shall set forth but two. The first is that the material we are told to keep confidential is *sacred,* in the same sense that the temple itself is sacred. Just as it makes sense that no unclean person should be allowed to enter the temple's holy precincts (see D&C 94:8-9), so it makes equal sense that no unclean mind should be given sacred information which might result in ridicule or profanation (see Matt. 13:13). The Savior forbade us to feed that which is holy to the dogs or to cast our pearls before swine (see Matt. 7:6). This was not said out of contempt for dogs or swine, but to emphasize that holy and extremely precious things are entitled to better treatment than to be chewed up by dogs or trampled in the mud by pigs. If we become careless in promiscuously scattering knowledge of these sacred things, who knows what spiritual filth they might land in?

The second reason for confidentiality is that knowledge of sacred things carries with it a heavy responsibility—perhaps heavier than most people are prepared to bear. In 2 Peter 2:20-21 we learn that if a person receives the truth and then forsakes it, it would have been better for him had he not received it at all. This same theme runs throughout the Book of Mormon and the Doctrine and Covenants: "For of him unto whom much is given much is required; and he who sins against the greater light shall receive the greater condemnation" (D&C 82:3). The Lord is doing many people a favor, rather than a disfavor, by withholding from them his sacred knowledge.

However, I am also convinced that the application of this principle of respecting confidentialities must not extend to things that are *not* confidential, lest we allow men and women to enter the temple totally uninformed and therefore unprepared. Giving too little information might be as improper as giving them too much. I recall one sister who was receiving her own endowment. In the middle of the session she arose and in an audible voice proclaimed, "Hey, I'm not ready for this," and turning around, she stalked out. Actually, I admired her honesty and courage, but regretted the circumstances that brought this about.

I feel it is morally wrong to authorize a person to receive his endowment without first being told that he will be required to make solemn covenants lasting for the rest of his life, and beyond, and that he would be held accountable to the Lord if he violates them. Failure to impress this upon his mind trivializes the ordinance itself. It unfairly places that person in moral jeopardy without giving him appropriate preparation or warning.

The Temple Preparation lessons approved by the First Presidency amply provide what is needed in this regard. The only danger today is that patrons might not receive these lessons, or might not fully understand them. The bishop or branch president who issues the temple recommend has a personal responsibility to be sure that the one receiving his own endowment has not only received full instructions on its seriousness but is sufficiently developed mentality to *understand its full import*. These delicate matters must remain the responsibility of the bishop or branch president and, of course, of the member of the stake presidency who countersigns the recommend. This is obligatory for all of them, because once the patron presents a valid temple recommend to the attendant at the front desk of the temple, the latter is required to admit him without further inquiry. The patron's worthiness is no longer under review. The temple is not an appellate body to review the judgments rendered by appropriate priesthood officers on the ward and stake level.

Now the question arises, does the rule of confidentiality still remain in force in view of the fact that some of these extremely confidential matters have already been wrongfully divulged to the world? Out of the countless persons who have come to the temple, it is inevitable, I suppose, that a handful of them might have refused to play by the rules, and might have done what they covenanted not to do. They will have to personally answer to the Lord for their perfidy. As far as the rest of us are concerned, do our lips still remain sealed? The answer to both of the above questions is, yes, the rule of secrecy still prevails, and yes, our lips do remain sealed.

It isn't just that the Lord doesn't want these sacred matters to fall onto profane ears, though that is important enough. An additional principle is involved—the Lord wants to know who among his faithful servants are strong-willed enough to respect their oaths of confidentiality. This is one of the qualities we must develop during our earthly experience as a prelude to earning the right to enlarge our knowledge.

The Prophet Joseph Smith once said, "The reason we do not have the secrets of the Lord revealed unto us, is because we do not keep them but reveal them; [if]we do not keep our own secrets, but reveal our difficulties to the world, even to our enemies, then how would we keep the secrets of the Lord? I can keep a secret till doomsday."[2]

The Prophet Joseph Smith was quite correct in stating that he was able to keep the Lord's secrets. For example, he never revealed to the world the mechanical process involved in his use of the Urim and

Thummim in translating the plates, other than explaining it in the most general terms. But the specific and intriguing details, which the world is hungry to receive, he never divulged. We can be quite certain that the Lord had forbidden him from doing so. Moreover, after that melancholy incident involving his reprimand from the Lord for the loss of the 116 pages of the Book of Mormon manuscript, he did not have to be told twice.

Patience in Learning the Things of God

The third point which I would cover in discussions with my interrogators is the need for patience in receiving the answers they are looking for. Without patience, they are inviting dreadful disappointment. Realizing that the Lord has refused to answer many of our nagging questions, we can take comfort in the assurance that some day he will (see D&C 101:32-34).

The children of Israel gave us a good example to follow in this regard. They were told by the Lord to perform blood sacrifices for fourteen hundred years, without having a clear idea of why they were doing it. It was an exercise of pure faith and patience. Their own scriptures were replete with references to the coming of their Messiah, whose atoning sacrifice these blood sacrifices foreshadowed, but the Jewish hierarchy apparently were unable, or unwilling, to link their blood sacrifices to their forthcoming Messiah's death. For them, the slaughtering of all those thousands of choice bulls and rams was a real sacrifice, economically as well as ritually, which they performed, but without understanding. Whatever else we may say about their failure to correctly read the signs and symbols given them, we must acknowledge that they showed great patience. From those few who *did* understand the true symbolism of the blood sacrifices, the Lord also required patience, for the time they awaited had not yet come.

Patience is not one of this age's identifying qualities. Thanks to the wizardry of modern technology, today we want answers to all our questions right now, laid out clearly in bold type. We spend billions to get that kind of immediate delivery. In the nation's staggering, multi-billion-dollar annual media blitz, the theme in every sales appeal is "instant gratification." Those two words seem to undergird almost everything we buy, or do, or think. But the Lord has told us that we must rid ourselves of this trivialized and unrealistic approach to the deep mysteries of eternity. Life's best fruit is slow-growing. We must adjust our thinking to accept the fact that the Lord is not yet ready to give us everything we want. Note his words on the subject: "I have yet many things to say unto you, but ye cannot bear them now" (John 16:12). And again: "Ye are not able to abide the presence of God now, neither the ministering of angels; wherefore, continue in patience until ye are perfected" (D&C 67:13).

The Lord's vision is infinite, while ours is comparatively microscopic. He has his own timetable. In fact, he has *multiple* timetables. For preaching the gospel and for doing our temple work, his timetable calls for *immediate* performance. Revealing to his children all the mysteries of the Kingdom, however, calls for *future* delivery. The following scripture will bring comfort to those who want assurance that someday their patience will be rewarded:

> Yea, verily I say unto you, in that day when the Lord shall come, he shall reveal all things—Things which have passed, and hidden things which no man knew, things of the earth, by which it was made, and the purpose and the end thereof—Things most precious [I believe that that includes the temple ordinances and their meaning], things that are above, and things that are beneath, things that are in the earth, and upon the earth, and in heaven (D&C 101:32-34).

I invite those who are interested in pursuing this point further to carefully read 3 Nephi 26:9, in conjunction with 2 Nephi 27:8-11. In the latter passage, the Lord tells us that the *entire* Book of Mormon, including the two-thirds of it still *remaining sealed,* reveals all things "from the foundation of the world unto the end thereof"(v. 10), but that the things that were sealed were withheld from us because of our "wickedness and abominations" (v. 8). The reason for giving us only one-third of the plates was to "try their [our] faith" (3 Ne. 26:9), which in turn tests our worthiness to later receive the entire package of answers to our questions, a point that the Lord does not want us to miss.

What, then, is the message of these scriptures? It is that we cannot expect the Lord to conform his cosmic plans to our puny time line. If we have patience, all things, including the undisclosed mysteries of the temple ordinances and much more, will eventually be made known.

Spiritual Exertion

The other side of this coin, however, must also be considered. If we were to push the application of the principle of patience to its outer limits, we would turn ourselves into an inert mass of spectators, reduced to sitting by the side of the road of life with our empty cup of knowledge in hand, waiting for the Lord to come along and fill it up. But that's not the way it is. Before he fills up our cup, he expects us first to do "all that we can do" (2 Nephi 25:23), recognizing, of course, that some have more resources to work with than others. We must first act upon the knowledge that he has already given us. To those who are waiting for further light from heaven, may I suggest that many of the answers to our quandaries are already available if we will put forth effort to find them. Latter-day Saints should remember that they have already received more information than any other people since before "the foundation of the world" (see D&C 124:41). The amount of knowledge we have accumulated is awesome. We are highly favored of the Lord in that respect and should never forget it.

To expand our knowledge of the revelations bearing upon the purpose and function of our temples, we should begin with a careful examination of our own scriptures, particularly the Doctrine and Covenants (sections 94, 97, 109, 110, 124, 127, 128, and 138). In addition, references in volumes 2, 3, and 4 of the *History of the Church* to the construction and use of the Kirtland and Nauvoo temples, numerous scriptural references to temples in the *Topical Index* in the LDS edition of the Bible, in the *Encyclopedia of Mormonism,* and countless other LDS source materials should be consulted. If one is ambitious enough to belong to the Foundation for Ancient Research and Mormon Studies (FARMS), he will have enough scholarly material available to keep him busy for the rest of his life.

If we sometimes complain of having to live in today's super-secular society, we should also consider the advantages of being able to retrieve incalculable quantities of information about temples and related subjects. Newly discovered apocryphal but reliable ancient scrolls and codices, archaeological diggings, and computer-driven research into the archives of modern temple history are at our fingertips. No other generation in history has had so much knowledge spread before it, a blessing we must not fail to appreciate. The Lord expects us to find and use this knowledge, for that is why it has been given to us. The oft-quoted passage in Joel (2:28-29) is very much relevant to this subject.

Through the efforts of our own LDS researchers, much historical data have been gathered and now lie within the "public domain." Academicians today have only to retrieve them, analyze them, and then play them back to the world in understandable form. This is precisely what our scholars are doing—with encouraging results. It's all very exciting, and has greatly enlarged our understanding of what temples are all about.

The Church too, has made conspicuous progress in preparing first-time endowment patrons for their new experience by giving them far more non-confidential information than it formerly did. The temple preparation courses previously approved by the First Presidency are excellent and comprehensive, and have made an enormous difference. Temple procedures have changed, by giving those receiving their own endowment a warm and loving reception, a personal escort throughout the unfolding of the ceremony, an orientation lecture (usually given by a member of the temple presidency), and other procedures designed to make this a pleasant and inspirational experience. The own-endowment patrons today feel better informed and more loved and cared for than ever before.

Conclusion

To summarize, we must say neither too much nor too little. The Lord will inspire us to do what is right if we follow his instructions. We should expand our understanding by using the resources already given us and prepare to receive whatever else the Lord may wish to give us, according to our needs and his designs.

2
Roots

Occasionally I see a young patron finish his first temple session a little glassy-eyed from sheer bewilderment. This is the symptom of a mild cultural shock for those whose two-dimensional view of the world keeps their imagination from wandering back into the exotic but fascinating world of the Old Testament. On the other hand, those who do have an Old Testament background are rewarded with a much better understanding of their temple experience. It should come as no surprise that today's temple ceremony, which I may compare to the branches of a tree, should have grown from its Old Testament roots. Note how the following scripture bears out this underlying principle of truth's uninterrupted continuity, ". . . neither doth he [God] vary from that which he hath said, therefore his paths are straight and his course is one eternal round" (see D&C 3:2). The corollary to that principle is that our understanding of God's unchanging truth continues to grow, even as our capacity to understand continues to grow.

The Lord builds the future on the foundation of the past, and his newest revelations are a seamless continuum of the revelations that preceded them. Note the following: "What I the Lord have spoken, I have spoken, and I excuse not myself; and though the heavens and the earth pass away, my word shall not pass away; but shall all be fulfilled. . . ." (D&C 1:38).

To characterize this principle, I have often used the term "revelatory continuity," meaning simply that when God gives a new revelation to his children, he couches it, where applicable, in the language of previous revelations. For example, the words of the Lord to the Prophet Joseph Smith in his first vision in the Sacred Grove: " . . . having a form of godliness, but they deny the power thereof" are a direct quotation from 2 Timothy 3:5. The Angel Moroni couched much—probably most—of his message of the restoration to the Prophet Joseph Smith in language taken directly from the Old and New Testaments. We note that in addition to the several biblical passages which we know Moroni quoted almost verbatim, he also "quoted many more passages of [biblical] scripture."[3] As a result, the foliage of the restored gospel became an outgrowth of its biblical roots (see also 3 Ne. 23:1-4). In order to be completely comfortable with the temple ordinances, one must first adjust his vision by taking in the entire panorama of creation encompassing the past, the present, and the future.

A brief review of the history of the Jewish temples and of ancient Jewish ceremonial practices will increase our understanding of present-day temple procedures. They may also help us to better understand what the Lord is telling us through the message of our modern temple ordinances. No direct comparisons are made between this historical material and any confidential portions of our present-day temple ordinances. The parallels between the ancient and the modern are there, but the reader is left to construct them in his mind by himself.

Definition of the Term "Temple" and Its Purpose

Historically, the term "temple" has been construed to mean any holy sanctuary where man and God could meet under very special circumstances. Temple worship has been practiced not only by worshippers of "the only true and living God," but by people of almost every age and culture since the dawn of human history. From the Latter-day Saint point of view, most worldwide temples were not "true temples" at all (that is, authorized to perform valid temple ordinances), but they nevertheless conformed to the historically accepted definition of a temple. They provided the site where men and women might draw closer to God in their own fashion and in a way not possible in their ordinary manner of worship. Historical temples also provided a site for performing sacred ceremonies (including blood sacrifices), for performing astronomical calculations, maintaining sacred libraries, and for teaching and training priests.

Today, many of these ancient temples are still intact in China and India, in Europe, North Africa, ancient America, and, of course, in the Middle East, which cradled many of the world's religions.

Many of these temples and their related ceremonies, apostate though they may have been, show certain architectural features and symbols which bear a resemblance to distinctive features of our own Latter-day Saint temples and ceremonies. Latter-day Saint scholars have recently made some startling discoveries in this regard. It is reasonable to surmise that the antecedents of these temples may originally have been intertwined with the history of "true temples," and that though they may have subsequently drifted off into apostasy, they still carry the vestigial remains of their authentic origins.

Because temples served the purpose of bringing men closer to God, it followed that their devotees felt that this would be more successfully accomplished on top of a high hill or mountain.[4] Where that was impossible, a tower or pyramid was often constructed and a temple placed on top. This, it is believed, was the purpose for erecting the Tower of Babel and the well-known pyramids in Mesoamerica. In the latter case, climbing the innumerable steps leading to the summit may have been intended to symbolize man's ascension to his final glory in God's exalted presence. Temples were often characterized as the world's "navel," since they were, symbolically, located mid-way between heaven and earth.[5]

These unauthorized temples have held a fascination for Latter-day Saint scholars because our record of *authorized* ancient temples is so sketchy, or nonexistent, during long historical periods. We find it useful, therefore, to resort to the history of unauthorized temples, many of whose remains are relatively easy to find, to help us fill in the gaps.

Concerning authorized, or "true" temples, we must first understand what they are. From the Latter-day Saint point of view, the term "true temple" minimally embodies two ideas. First, it is a sacred building where man and God can meet in an especially secure and sacred environment. Second, it is the place where sacred priesthood ordinances can be performed under God's special authorization.

The Temples' Origins

How far back in history can we trace these temple ordinances? Apparently, all the way back to the beginning. In Moses 5:59 we read: "And thus all things were confirmed unto Adam, by an *holy ordinance. . . .*" From the context, it is reasonable to interpret the words "holy ordinance" to mean "temple ordinance." From that we may conclude that Adam and Eve knew of, and presumably participated in, temple ordinances comparable to our own, excluding work for the dead, as will be explained later. We have been authoritatively told that the ordinances given to Adam continued until the time of Moses and thereafter, and were continued up until the time of Christ.

From Adam down to Moses, however, we find no mention of any building matching our definition of what a temple really is. It is true that Noah, Abraham, Isaac, Jacob and others are all mentioned as having built altars to the Lord, which no doubt involved blood sacrifices, and which we may consider as forerunners of later temple ordinances. These activities, too, can legitimately be called "temple experiences."

The Nephites, living subsequently to Moses, also had temples, although their function is not fully explained. President Joseph Fielding Smith confirms the idea of the non-existence of true temples during the period from Adam to Moses in the following words:

> We have no record of the building of temples before the flood nor for several centuries following. This lack of information does not mean that such sacred structures were not known. During the years when a temple could not be built, the servants of the Lord went to the mountaintops to communicate with the Lord. It was on the top of a mountain that Enoch spoke with the Lord. It was on the mountain that Moses did likewise, as did Nephi and the Brother of Jared.[6]

As stated above, Adam and Eve presumably became acquainted with, and participated in, temple ordinances and covenants, even though no mention is made of a specific building. Chapter five in the Book of Moses is of the greatest importance for our purposes, for it is there that we also learn that the Lord directed Adam to offer up blood sacrifices (vv. 5-8), and that "This thing is a similitude of the sacrifice of the Only Begotten of the Father, which is full of grace and truth" (v. 7).

From these verses which are, significantly, grouped together into one chapter, we learn that: (1) the Savior was to offer himself up as a sacrifice for the sins of all mankind, (2) Adam (and presumably his righteous posterity) were to continue to offer up blood sacrifices as a similitude of this one great sacrifice, (although many of the children of Israel, who later continued to offer up blood sacrifices, were presumably unaware of the reason for it even though God, through Moses, had commanded them to do so), and, (3) temple ordinances as we understand them today were also made known at the very beginning as a type and shadow of the atoning sacrifice of our Lord and Savior. The fact that present-day temple ordinances are also oriented toward the Savior, his great sacrifice and his creative role, has been confirmed by our modern prophets.

We can, at this point, legitimately ask ourselves at least this one question: Were the ordinances which were performed in the tabernacle, or the temple of Solomon, identical to those performed in modern-day temples? In the Doctrine and Covenants we read: "For, for this cause I commanded Moses that he should build a tabernacle, . . . and to build a house in the land of promise, that those ordinances might be revealed which had been hid from before the world was" (see D&C 124:38). This suggests that sacred ordinances may have been performed in the tabernacle, and later, presumably in the temples, which were successors to the tabernacle.

A further question which might be asked, however, is whether those ordinances, if indeed they were administered there, included ordinances on behalf of the dead, such as are administered in today's temples. The answer would have to be, unequivocally, no. Administering ordinances for the dead is a function of the Melchizedek priesthood, whereas the Jewish temple officiators held only the priesthood of Aaron (see D&C 84:25-27). President Joseph Fielding Smith had the following to say on this subject, "In this dispensation, the temple work is under the direction of the Melchizedek Priesthood . . ."[7] (see D&C 84:19-29: "And this greater [Melchizedek] priesthood administereth the gospel and holdeth the key of the mysteries of the kingdom, even the key of the knowledge of God. Therefore, *in the ordinances thereof,* the power of godliness is manifest").

From the writings of President Joseph Fielding Smith:

> There is nothing recorded in the Old Testament declaring that gospel ordinances were performed in the Temple of Solomon in the interest of the dead. In all that was written in the Old Testament, or in the Book of Mormon pertaining to the history of Israel, nothing in any manner conveys the thought that vicarious work was performed in those early times for the dead. Until the Son of God had finished his preparations for the salvation of man and to bring to pass the resurrection of the dead, there

could be no ordinance or labor of any kind pertaining to the resurrection and redemption of mankind that could be performed for the dead. Therefore, in the Temple of Solomon the ordinances were confined to the living.[8]

The Tabernacle in the Wilderness and Subsequent Temples

We now come to the famed tabernacle in the wilderness, about whose architectural features we know much, but about whose functions we know less. Though we sometimes refer to it as the first authentic temple about which we have any reliable information, the fact is that it wasn't really a temple at all, but a portable structure—a tent which could be set up, taken down, and carried from place to place at will. But functionally, if not structurally, we must consider it as the mother of all subsequent authentic temples constructed from that time right up to the present day.

After the children of Israel escaped from Egyptian captivity and reached the Sinai wilderness, the construction of the tabernacle became almost the first item on the Lord's agenda. The tabernacle's principal function was to provide a site for the Ark of the Covenant, or Ark of the Testimony, which was to be installed in the Most Holy Place, the tabernacle's innermost chamber. The mercy seat served as the Ark's lid, or covering, and was veneered with a layer of pure gold. Its importance lay in the fact that it represented God's throne, where he could come down and meet with Moses and talk with him, as one man talks with another (Ex. 25:22). And so, from the very beginning, the tabernacle was viewed as the sacred spot where God's presence could be felt in a way possible nowhere else on earth. This was not to take place in some jerry-built structure but rather in one of splendid refinement, built exactly according to God's specifications.

It is enlightening at this point to quote a few verses from the 25th chapter of Exodus, which refer to the construction of the tabernacle and its *raison d'être*.

> And the Lord spake unto Moses, saying, speak unto the children of Israel that they bring me an offering: of every man that giveth it willingly with his heart ye shall take my offering. (vv. 1-2)

In other words, the Lord wanted the tabernacle to be built from the free-will offerings of the people.

> And this is the offering which ye shall take of them; gold, and silver, and brass . . . (v. 3)

This was actually bronze.

> And blue, and purple, and scarlet, . . . (v. 4).

These colors are highly symbolic. Blue represented the sky, and therefore heaven and obedience to God. It was also a symbol of peace. Purple was the most expensive of all the dyes or colors [made from crushed beetles] and became the symbol of royalty and of the honor due to the Messiah-to-come, the King of Israel. Scarlet was symbolic of the blood to be shed by the Savior for the sins of the world. Note that everything about the tabernacle was symbolic.

> . . . and fine linen and goats' hair, and rams' skins dyed red, and badgers' skins, and shittim wood, oil for the light, spices for anointing oil, and for sweet incense, . . . (vv. 4-6)

Note the parallelism between the Lord's asking the Israelites to contribute the finest of their treasure to the construction of the tabernacle and the Lord's directing modern-day Israel to contribute the finest of their treasure for the building of the Nauvoo temple (see D&C 124:26-28). Note also that today's temples represent the finest workmanship of which the Church is capable.

The above facts, incidentally, contradict the popular stereotype of the children of Israel, which portrays them as an undisciplined mob of ragged runaway slaves, without property, education, or skills of any kind beyond that of brick-making. The text paints quite a different picture. They obviously had enough wealth to amass a considerable quantity of the most expensive of building materials, including gold and silver in large quantities, and bronze, and many precious stones, and fine-twined linens, and expensive dyes, and costly and exotic timber. They certainly must have counted among their numbers many skilled and well-trained craftsmen and artists capable of satisfying the most complex and exacting instructions by the Lord to produce a structure of unequaled workmanship.

> And let them make me a sanctuary;

This has reference to the tabernacle itself,

> that I may dwell among them. (v. 8)

These are the key words. The Tabernacle was to be a place where God could come down and communicate, person to person, with his children:

> . . . And they shall make me an ark of shittim wood: two cubits and a half shall be the length thereof, and a cubit and a half in breadth thereof, and a cubit and a half the height thereof. (v. 10)

The length of a cubit was presumably eighteen inches. We are told here that the Ark of the Covenant was about three and three-quarters feet long and two and one-quarter feet wide, as well as high. It was the most sacred object in all of Israel.

> And thou shalt overlay it with pure gold, within and without shalt thou overlay it, and shall make upon it a crown of gold round about. (v. 11)

Nothing was too good for the Lord. It is obvious that constructing the tabernacle called for skilled craftsmen and artisans of the highest order.

> And thou shalt cast four rings of gold for it, and put them in the four corners thereof; and two rings shall be in the one side of it, and two rings in the other side of it. (v. 12)

That was important. The rings were intended to accommodate the insertion of two staves so that the Ark could be transported without man's ever touching it. The Ark was absolutely untouchable except under very special circumstances; anybody wrongfully violating this injunction brought down the severest divine wrath upon his head (see 2 Sam. 6:6-7).

> And thou shalt make a mercy seat of pure gold: two cubits and a half shall be the length thereof, and a cubit and a half the breadth thereof. (v. 17)

The importance of the Ark of the Covenant was certainly not measured by its size, which was relatively tiny, but by its sanctity. This was also true of the tabernacle itself, whose size, comparatively speaking, was minuscule.

The mercy seat was the covering or the lid placed over the Ark of the Covenant. On the mercy seat were two cherubim. We don't know exactly who, or what, they were. Presumably they were the effigies of two diminutive angels because the text does refer to their faces. They were positioned on the mercy seat, presumably kneeling, facing each other with their overarching wings touching. The text, however, does not give us the details as to their identity. One must draw his own conclusions.

The Israelites were almost fanatical in their insistence on protecting sacred places from defilement. It is said that when the High Priest entered the Most Holy Place in Solomon's Temple a cord was attached to his sash, with the other end extending out into the next room. If he should suffer a heart attack, his assistants could drag him out rather than enter the sacred precincts where they had no right to go.

The Israelites also laid far greater emphasis than we do on the special honor extended to sacred vestments and physical objects associated with their acts of worship. They also considered the names of individuals to be of great importance. The general practice in Israel was to give a child one name only. That name indicated a quality or characteristic which the child hopefully would embody. The selection of a name was therefore something taken most seriously. All of these attitudes are cultural characteristics, familiarity with which will assist us to better appreciate the modern temple ordinances. Our present generation, fortunately or unfortunately (depending on one's point of view) places far less emphasis on the sanctity of names, vestments, places, or icons of worship than did our forebears; but one thing is certain: to fully understand the present-day temple practices, one must understand that the religious practices out of which they grew reflected a mentality which placed special respect for sacred things at the very heart of their worship.

In the rest of Exodus 25, as well as elsewhere, the Lord gives further details concerning the tabernacle and its appurtenances, but there is no need, at this point, to explore the matter further. One further verse in Exodus 25 is worthy of special attention, however, because it epitomizes all that was said above concerning God's presence at the mercy seat:

> And there will I meet with thee, and I will commune with thee from above the mercy seat, from between the two cherubims which are upon the ark of the testimony, of all things which I will give thee in commandment unto the children of Israel (v. 22).

In Exodus 33:9 we find a fulfillment of God's promise that he would rendezvous with man in the tabernacle. "And it came to pass, as Moses entered into the tabernacle, the cloudy pillar descended, and stood at the door of the tabernacle, and the Lord talked with Moses." The term "cloudy pillar" requires an explanation because the translation from the Hebrew is misleading. Actually, what was referred to was a column of dazzlingly brilliant light rather than a cover of dark, moisture-laden rain clouds.[9] Finally, verse 10 of Exodus 33 reads, "And all the people saw the cloudy pillar stand at the tabernacle door: and all the people rose up and worshiped, every man in his tent door."

The construction of the tabernacle in the wilderness was finally accomplished according to the Lord's strict instructions. To ensure its physical safety, and to protect its sanctity, representatives of the tribes of Israel were so encamped as to totally surround it, thus causing it to be "fenced off" from the rest of the world. In this way, access to its sacred precincts was strictly controlled to avoid any possible defilement by errant intruders.

A comparable result is accomplished today in connection with our own temples—not by placing a ring of armed guards around them to keep out the intruders—but by first submitting its patrons to a rigorous temple recommend interview. This has the same effect of protecting the temple's sanctity against unwanted guests.

In Exodus 28, and elsewhere, we are told of various articles of clothing worn by the priests in administering the temple ceremonies. We note, for example, reference to the "breastplate of judgment" (v. 30). The *LDS Bible Dictionary* informs us that there were actually two entirely different articles of attire mentioned in the Old and New Testament answering to the English designation "breastplate." One of them was a piece of armor intended to protect a soldier's upper torso in battle (Ephesians 6:14). The other was an article of clothing to be worn by the high priest in the execution of his office.[10]

The latter was "made of linen, colorfully arranged, bearing 12 precious stones and the Urim and Thummim."[11] This is of the greatest of interest to the Latter-day Saints as the Prophet Joseph Smith is very specific that inside the stone cavity in which he found the gold plates he also found the Urim and Thummim and the breastplate, both of which played a cardinal role in the translation of the Book of Mormon.[12] Elsewhere[13] the Prophet tells us that "there were two stones in silver bows—and these stones, fastened to a breastplate, constituted what is called the Urim and Thummim. . . ."

This explanation may possibly throw light on a well-known mystery, namely: what could be the linkage between a piece of armor and the translation of sacred records? Moreover, how can one conveniently fasten two stones to a piece of armor? Searching for an answer, let us postulate that the "breastplate" of Book of Mormon fame might have been an *article of temple clothing,* worn by the high priest on special ceremonial occasions, and made of linen. This might make it easier to visualize the breastplate's function and its relation to the Urim and Thummim, of which it was a part. This is only a supposition, however, and no one can be dogmatic on this point because the Prophet Joseph Smith refrained from providing us with further clarification. Some of the available evidence, moreover, suggests a contrary conclusion.

We are told of an "ephod" (Ex. 28:6) which was also an article of clothing worn by the high priest and perhaps other priests. It was "shaped like a waistcoat with two shoulder pieces and a girdle. It was of richly variegated material, blue, purple and scarlet. On the shoulder pieces were two onyx stones on which were engraved the names of the 12 tribes. To the ephod was fastened the Breastplate of Judgment."[14]

Reference is also made to a "robe" (Ex. 28:4) which we can translate "tunic"; a "mitre" (v. 4), which we can translate "crown" or "turban"; a "girdle" (v. 4) which translates "sash"; and "ouches" (v. 13) which translates as a "setting for a precious stone."[15]

Almost everything connected with the tabernacle was symbolic and designed to emphasize the fact that entering into the presence of God was the most solemn and serious thing a person could do, and was not to be trivialized or passed over lightly.

Surrounding the tabernacle was an area generally referred to as the tabernacle court, composed of both an outer and an inner court. This was the area that was "fenced off," with the Tabernacle positioned toward the middle. Access to it, like that to the the tabernacle itself, was also restricted to those whose eligibility had been previously certified according to their worthiness and their assigned function. The only access to the court was through an elaborately designed entrance way. There was no back door or side door, nor could one legally climb over the fence. This simple fact was, in itself, highly symbolic. Compare "He that entereth not by the door into the sheepfold, but climbeth up some other way, the same is a thief and a robber" (John 10:1). The parallelism to modern temples ordinances is left to the imagination of the reader.

What were the dimensions of the tabernacle and its outer court? Assuming the length of a cubit to have been eighteen inches, the combined outer and inner tabernacle courts must have been 150 feet long, and 75 feet wide, or the equivalent of one-half the length and width, respectively, of a modern football field. The tabernacle itself was also in the form of a rectangle, forty-five feet long, fifteen feet wide, and fifteen feet high. It was subdivided into two chambers, designated as the Holy Place, which measured thirty feet in length, and fifteen feet in width and height; and the Most Holy Place (first called the "Holy of Holies" by John Milton), which measured fifteen feet in length, width, and height. In other words, it formed a perfect cube.

What impresses one is the fact that the Tabernacle was so small. More than 88 of them could have been placed inside the Washington D.C. temple. Even the three dimensions of the later temple of Solomon were a modest thirty by thirty by ninety feet, or, in other words, double the three dimensions of the tabernacle. One might add, whimsically, that if the tabernacle had been tucked away somewhere inside the cavernous Basilica of St. Peter's in Rome, pilgrims would have found it only with great difficulty. This fact has doctrinal significance because it emphasizes that in measuring the significance of a sacred temple, sanctity is more important than dimensions. We note in this connection the words of Elder Boyd K. Packer of the Council of the Twelve: "It is not the building itself but the visitations of the Spirit that sanctifies. When the people stray from the Spirit their sanctuary ceases to be the house of the Lord."[16]

For a more accurate understanding of the English New Testament, one must make a distinction between two Greek-language words which have different meanings, both of which are translated into the single English word "temple." One of those words is *naos*, which refers to the temple building itself and to the court immediately surrounding it, access to which was reserved only to a small and especially designated priestly coterie. This was the area invested with the utmost sanctity.

In contrast, the temple of Solomon, built 450 years later, as well as its successor Zerubbabel and Herod temples, in addition to the *naos,* also provided for a much larger temple area, or outer court, which extended far beyond the boundaries of the above-mentioned *naos,* and access to which was much less restricted. Recent excavations have shown, for example, that this outer fringe area, which in Greek was referred to as the *hieron,* and to which we find frequent reference in connection with the Temple of Herod, was accessible, at least in part, even to gentiles.

This would never have been permitted in the days of Moses. Yet this enlarged area was still considered to be part of the "temple" and was given that appellation in the New Testament.

When referring to it, however, the Greek word *hieron,* rather than *naos,* was used; in English this distinction disappears and both the larger and smaller areas are referred to as the "temple." How does one tell the difference? He must rely on the context, or refer back to the original Greek text.

The importance of this point cannot be exaggerated. In the New Testament the Savior went into the temple to teach (John 8:20), or to drive out the money changers (John 2:15), or to watch the people cast their money into the treasury (Mark 12:41).[17] From these references we can reasonably conclude that an unrestrained going-and-coming existed in this enlarged area of the temple, not unlike a modern market place. Just the one English word "temple" also covers that particular meaning. This can create confusion, because this interpretation is so inconsistent with what we have learned about the exclusiveness of the inner temple court. We have no record of the Savior's ever having entered the latter, i.e., the *naos*.

Let us go back to the tabernacle and its surrounding court to learn the nature of the sacred artifacts placed there that God considered essential to Israelite worship. We will note that every one of these sacred objects was a "type and shadow" (i.e., that which foreshadowed or symbolically pointed to something yet to come).

If we had had access to the Tabernacle court over three thousand years ago, what would we have seen? The first object to have met our eyes would have been the altar of sacrifice where daily holocausts were performed by the Levites on behalf of Israel. Without going into a full explanation of the extremely complex nature of these various sacrifices, the following point helps give meaning to these bloody immolations which, to modern sensitivities, seem almost repulsive. The sacrificial victim, usually a bull or ram, had been previously selected because of its total absence of physical defects. Christians generally (and definitely including the Latter-day Saints) understand that the victim's physical perfection symbolically typified the perfection of the "Lamb of God." The shedding of its blood was a similitude of the shedding of the blood of their Lord and Savior, which was, in the words of Elder Bruce R. McConkie (referring to the Atonement), "the most important single thing that has ever occurred in the entire history of created things."[18]

Behind the altar of sacrifice was a large basin of water, sometimes called the laver (the English word being taken directly from the French verb "laver," meaning "to wash"). The Temple of Solomon had a much larger basin called the "Molten Sea," measuring 15 feet in diameter and 7½ feet deep (see 1 Kgs. 7:23). The use of smaller "lavers," however, was also continued in Solomon's temple, but they were mobile, being equipped with wheels. The purpose of this large accumulation of fresh water (in a land where, during the dry season, water was extremely hard to obtain) was to provide the Levites and priests the wherewithal to wash themselves, both before and after performing their sacrificial duties. With a little imagination, we can picture the conditions confronting the officiators, which required such elaborate ablutions. Crimson blood flowed in rivulets and was accompanied no doubt by swarms of flies and the all-pervasive stench of burnt and rotting flesh and of sweat brought on by the heat of the scorching desert sun. Obviously, this ablution was indispensable for hygienic and esthetic, as well as ceremonial, purposes. The curious reader is referred to the material appearing under the heading "Sacrifices" on page 765 of the *LDS Bible Dictionary.*

Those who see in the laver a precursor to our modern-day baptismal font will find supportive evidence somewhat equivocal. The common feature of these two objects is their use of water, whose use has always been associated with purification. But whereas our present-day baptismal fonts are involved exclusively in a symbolic purification, the function of the laver was much broader. All of the four evangelists refer to the baptism of Jesus by John the Baptist with very little background explanation. Can we infer that they assumed that the reader already possessed information about this sacred ordinance, which must have come from somewhere? If so, then from where? This is still an open question.

Having discussed the two most conspicuous items in the outer court, let us now consider the "Holy Place" (not to be confused with the "Most Holy Place," or "Holy of Holies," just beyond it). To the right was the "table of the shewbread," which was a table made of acacia wood and overlaid with gold. On top of it were placed twelve "cakes," or loaves of unleavened shewbread, arranged in two piles of six each, and representing the twelve tribes of Israel. The name "shewbread," or its equivalent in Hebrew, means "bread of the face," or "presence bread." Thus the shewbread recalled God's divine presence within the Tabernacle. The bread was unleavened for the reason that only that which was pure could endure the presence of God; leaven was considered impure.

Some historical evidence suggests that a vessel of wine may have rested on top of the loaves, although the biblical text is silent on this point. This bread was considered of the utmost sanctity, and only the priests could eat it, which they did once every week. The bread was then replaced, to be consumed the following week. A reasonable case can be made to support the position that this ceremony constituted a precursor to today's sacrament.

This also recalls the Old Testament episode in which David, during his earlier years, arrived at the tabernacle on one occasion in a starving condition. The priests apparently took pity on him and gave him some of the shewbread to eat. Though doing this was technically improper, the priests apparently felt that the requirements of mercy and charity overruled the requirements of scrupulous legal conformity (see 1 Sam. 21:6). The Savior of mankind referred to this episode in justifying his plucking the ears of corn (actually, heads of grain—probably wheat) on the Sabbath day (see Matthew 12:4). The question there was not whether Jesus had the right to help himself to the wheat, which the law of Moses allowed him to do under those circumstances, but whether he had the right to do it on the Sabbath day.

Passing over to the left side of the room, we would see a candelabrum called the menorah, made of gold, with seven branches. At the extremity of each was an oil-containing cup with a lighted wick. The menorah served the purpose of affording light to a room which otherwise would be in virtual darkness. However, it also performed a symbolic function. The word menorah actually refers to "a place of lights." We see it also as a symbol of spiritual light, and possibly, also, of the Holy Ghost.

In the center of the chamber, close to the veil that gives access to the Holy of Holies, was the altar of incense. That was the same altar before which Zacharias appeared fourteen hundred years later when he was visited by the Angel Gabriel, who told him of the forthcoming birth of his son John (the Baptist) (Luke 1:5-25). In those days, an authorized priest who had been previously selected by lot, entered that sacred chamber every day to place fuel and frankincense on the eternal flame, that it might never die.

The smoke from the fire symbolized an eternal prayer ascending to heaven and foreshadowed the Savior's great intercessory prayer (John 17:1-26). In fact, in the 141st Psalm we have specific reference to the link between this incense floating heavenward and our own prayers ascending to heaven: "Let my prayer be set forth before thee as incense; and the lifting up of my hands as the evening sacrifice" (Psalms 141:2).

In addition to the smoke's highly symbolic meaning, it had a practical use as well. The smoke tended to obscure the vision of the one standing before it and thus lessened the possibility of his inadvertently seeing through an accidental aperture in the veil behind it and feasting his eyes on the forbidden things that lay inside.

Having discussed the three sacred objects in the holy place, we are now ready to consider the Most Holy Place or the "Holy of Holies," wherein only the high priest was permitted to go, and then, only once a year. This little chamber formed a fifteen-foot cube, and in it was positioned the Ark of the Covenant. Other than that, it was empty.

In the *LDS Bible Dictionary* we read that the Holy of Holies contained only one piece of furniture: the Ark of the Covenant, or the Ark of the Testimony (Ex. 25:22). Within it rested "the testimony," i.e., the two tables of stone (Ex. 25:2l; 31:18).[19] According to Hebrews 9:4 it also contained a pot of manna and Aaron's rod that budded. However, these last two items apparently were not in the Ark at the time of Solomon (1 Kgs. 8:9). Upon the Ark and forming its lid was the mercy seat. It served, with the ark beneath it, as an altar on which the highest atonement known to the Jewish law was effected. On it was sprinkled the blood of the sin offering of the Day of Atonement (Lev. 16:14-15). The mercy seat was the place of the manifestation of "God's glory" (see Ex.25:22). It was God's throne in Israel. At its two extremities were placed two cherubim of beaten [gold] work, spreading their wings to cover the mercy seat.

On the Day of Atonement the high priest brought into the Most Holy Place a container of blood taken from a bull which had just been sacrificed. having first been specially consecrated to the purpose of wiping out the sins of Israel. By smearing this blood upon the Ark of the Covenant, the high priest symbolically covered over and expiated the combined sins of Israel. The analogy between this act and expiating, or covering over, the sins of humanity by the Savior's shedding of his blood on the cross is too perfect to be ignored or disbelieved.

Temples Subsequent to the Tabernacle

We will now briefly touch on a few subsequent episodes of Old Testament history relating to our temple theme. During much of the subsequent history, the Ark played both a mystical role and a significant role in the unfolding of historical events. For example, after the children of Israel's 40-year odyssey through the Sinai desert, the time came to enter the promised land. In crossing over the bed of the Jordan River (which had miraculously become dry), they were instructed to include the Ark of the Covenant in the procession around the beleaguered city of Jericho. Then, after encircling the city six times, with the ark still in their midst, and, on the seventh time around, after blasting on their trumpets seven times, the walls of the city fell with a mighty roar. Jehovah had brought them victory, and the Ark was recognized as the symbol of God's willingness to prosper the Israelites in material ways, on condition of their continued faithfulness.

On another occasion the Ark was stolen by the Philistines, resulting in their being smitten with a devastating plague. The story of Uzzah has even given us a new term for our English vocabulary. As the story goes, the Ark was being transported by oxen when one of them stumbled, threatening the Ark's safety. A certain Uzzah reached out to steady it. The Lord, in his displeasure at this sacrilege, thereupon sent down a bolt of lightning and Uzzah was smitten. Thus, "steadying the ark"now has the meaning of going beyond our authority in trying to rectify a wrong.

A little prior to the year 1,000 BC, the Temple of Solomon was constructed to afford the Ark a permanent resting place, and much has since been written about this historic event. The sacred text informs us that this new building was a sumptuous edifice indeed, whose renown soon spread throughout the known world. For its construction, cedar trees were brought down from Lebanon in large numbers, and other items were assembled from other localities, including expensive building materials, as well as metals, particularly gold and silver for ornamental and decorative work. The temple, which required more than seven years to build, seems to have been accorded the same world-wide level of notoriety as is accorded the present-day Taj Mahal. Yet, surprisingly, it was not a large building at all, as was previously pointed out. Actually it measured thirty by thirty by ninety feet. The Salt Lake Tabernacle, by contrast, measures two hundred fifty feet long by one hundred fifty feet wide, by eighty feet in height, which makes it 37 times larger.

Apparently, a large number of smaller annexes and appurtenances were included in the overall building complex. The various exterior courts were extended, and the temple approaches were built up, requiring the construction of roads and retaining walls. Moreover, the appurtenances were big and lavish. As previously said, the molten sea was fifteen feet in diameter, and seven-and-one-half feet deep. Special mention is made in the Old Testament of the temple's ornate furnishings and of the gorgeous gold and silver platters, cups, vessels, and candelabra constituting part of its inventory of sacred objects. Present were two tall free-standing pillars in front. One was named Jachen, meaning "He will establish," and the other, Boaz, meaning "in him is strength."

A few verses of the Old Testament text remain our principal source of information regarding this amazing building (although Flavius Josephus, the secular historian, also had much to say about it). From the book of 1 Kings, 6th chapter, we read:

> And the word of the Lord came to Solomon, saying, Concerning this house which thou art in building, if thou wilt walk in my statutes, and execute my judgments, and keep all my commandments to walk in them; then will I perform my word with thee, which I spake unto David thy father: And I will dwell among the children of Israel, and will not forsake my people Israel. So Solomon built the house, and finished it (vv. 11-14).

The Lord made a promise. If you keep this building sacred, he says, and follow all of my commandments, then I will be with you and with your children.

Skipping to chapter 8 of the same book of 1 Kings, starting with the first verse:

> Then Solomon assembled the elders of Israel, and all the heads of the tribes, the chief of the fathers of the children of Israel, unto King Solomon in Jerusalem, that they might bring up the ark of the covenant of the Lord to the city of David. . . . And all the men of Israel assembled themselves unto King Solomon at the feast in the month of Ethanim, which is the seventh month. And all the elders of Israel came, and the priests took up the ark. And they brought up the ark of the Lord, and the tabernacle of the congregation, and all the holy vessels that were in the tabernacle, even those did the priests and the Levites bring up. And King Solomon, and all the congregation of Israel, that were assembled unto him, were with him before the ark, sacrificing sheep and oxen, that could not be told nor numbered for multitude (vv. 1-5).

This passage paints a picture for us of a holocaust of gargantuan proportions, as the children of Israel showed their appreciation to the Lord for making possible this historic occurrence. It is apparent also that the scribes who recorded these events wanted the world to know just how big a sacrifice Israel had made for the temple and how big a celebration they held to commemorate its completion.

Following that came the consecration of the temple itself, to which they had been looking forward for more than seven years, and whose construction had cost them so much in effort and treasure:

> And the priests brought in the ark of the covenant of the Lord unto his place, into the oracle of the house, to the most holy place, even under the wings of the cherubim . . . There was nothing in the ark save the two tables of stone, which Moses put there at Horeb, . . . And it came to pass, when the priests were come out of the holy place, that the cloud filled the house of the Lord, so that the priests could not stand to minister because of the cloud: for the glory of the Lord had filled the house of the Lord (vv. 6, 9-11).

An apparent inconsistency exists here in that we learn elsewhere that originally the Ark of the Covenant had contained not only the tables on which the law was inscribed, but also a pot containing the manna that the Lord had given to the Israelites during the 40 years in the wilderness, and also the rod of Aaron, which had come into full flower under miraculous conditions. Apparently these additional items had become lost during the approximately four-hundred-and-fifty year interval.

In verse 11 we learn that the priests could not stand to minister because of "*the cloud: for the glory of the Lord had filled the house of the Lord.*" On this great day, the day of the dedication of this wonderful temple, which had cost Israel so much in national treasure, the glory of the Lord was there, indicating that Israel knew that the great Jehovah was looking down with approval and that their sacrifice had been accepted.

One can hardly avoid comparing this dazzling event with the events accompanying the dedication of the Kirtland Temple. The journal of the Prophet Joseph Smith comments on what happened on that occasion dated March 27, 1836:

> David Whitmer also saw an angel in the house. . . . President Brigham Young gave a short address in tongues and David W. Patten interpreted; and then gave a short exhortation in tongues, himself. . . . George A. Smith arose and began to prophesy, when a noise was heard like the sound of a rushing mighty wind, which filled the temple; . . .

> all the congregation arose . . . and many began to speak in tongues and prophesy; others saw glorious visions, and I beheld the temple was filled with angels . . . The people in the neighborhood came running . . . and were astonished at what was taking place.[20]

We can see the parallel between those two spectacular events. Unfortunately, the temple of Solomon became apostate soon thereafter, as did the Kirtland temple. Few of the wonderful things that the Lord promised for the temple of Solomon came to pass. Two or three hundred years later it became so defiled that it could no longer be considered worthy to administer the sacred ordinances which had been confided to it.

To give just one example of the sacrilege to which the temple was subjected, we are told that King Ahaz, one of the kings of Judah, reigning some 250 years after Solomon, had the effrontery to invade the temple and to order some of its most precious and sacred objects turned over to the King of Assyria, . . . a heathen and an arch enemy to Israel. This was the ultimate sacrilege. (2 Kgs. 16:8).

The above episode has an interesting modern-day parallel, but with a happier ending. In 1992 some renovations were made in the Washington D. C. Temple, which required replacing several thousand square feet of original carpeting. A number of Latter-day Saints, with the best of intentions, made application to purchase a few square feet of this discarded material, but the Church authorities wisely decided against it. In his temple dedicatory prayer in 1974, President Kimball had consecrated to the Lord, not only the building itself, but all of its appurtenances, including the furniture, the drapes, the carpets—everything. And so it was reasoned that dedicating a sacred object to the service of the Lord must be given meaning, and that placing it in a position where it might eventually be bought and sold in the commercial markets would be entirely inconsistent with its special status by virtue of its having been dedicated to the Lord. Property does change hands, and the decision of the Brethren was sound.

After the children of Israel were taken into Babylonian captivity by Nebuchadnezzar, his successor, Belshazzar, on one occasion held a lavish feast. For the delectation of his guests, he brought out the sacred golden vessels which had been plundered from Solomon's temple at the time of the conquest. Out of nowhere, there suddenly appeared a hand, which traced upon the wall for all to see, the words: MENE, MENE, TEKEL, UPHARSIN (see Dan. 5:25). No one there assembled, not even the King's astrologers or magicians, could interpret the message. The Prophet Daniel was then summoned, who informed the king that because of his sacrilege his time had come, and that e'er long, his empire would be destroyed. The prophesy proved to be on target. That night, Belshazzar was murdered, and soon thereafter the Persians overran the Babylonian empire.

The great temple of Solomon, the pride and glory of Israel, in behalf of which such wonderful promises had been made by the Lord himself, became desolate. His spirit had withdrawn itself, which meant that when it was pillaged and destroyed by the Babylonians, the Lord refused to lift a finger to save it. At the temple's dedication the Lord had specifically promised Solomon that if he, Solomon, who was acting symbolically on behalf of all of Israel, would walk in integrity of heart and in uprightness, and do according to all that the Lord had commanded him to do, then his eyes and heart would be there (i.e., in the temple) perpetually, and Solomon's, and his successors', reign, would continue forever (see 1 Kgs. 9:1-10). What actually happened during the following four centuries, however, was that the Jews did few of the things that God commanded them to do, and consequently they received few of the blessings that God had conditionally promised to give them.

Cyrus, the Persian emperor, whose armies had utterly dismembered the Babylonian empire, allowed the children of Israel to return to their home. There they rebuilt the temple, known as the temple of Zerubbabel, which, after about 400 years, again fell into disrepair.

The Temple of Herod

It was the responsibility of King Herod the Great, who died shortly after the birth of the Savior, to rebuild the temple, which he started to do, although it wasn't finished until long after his death. The results were good, even though his motives were bad. Although the New Testament portrays him as a fiendish monster, which he certainly was (Matthew 2:16), he did have unusual talents for organizing and building, and the appellation "the Great" was not entirely inappropriate.

Tourists today are awed by hearing the long list of his successful construction ventures, many of which are still visible. For example, he built the seaport at Joppa (present-day Jaffa), which transformed Judea into a maritime nation. He also built the palace and fortification on the plateau of Masada, as well as many other equally impressive works. Finally, his constructing the temple (which continued long after his death) gave him celebrity status, even though his reputation as a moral individual had become deservedly tarnished. This temple was the one frequented by the Savior, and from which he drove the money changers. He did acknowledge it, however, to be "My Father's house" (see John 2:16).

One further aspect of Herod's undertaking should be mentioned, for it carries with it important implications today. In addition to rebuilding the temple, Herod also included in his construction plans a southern extension of the outer temple court. It will be remembered that the temple was built on Mount Moriah (see 2 Chr. 3:1) whose general topography was irregular. The surface of the ground, starting at the temple itself, sloped downward to the south. That meant that to enlarge the area of the outer temple court to the south and west required a massive south and west retaining wall, plus tens of thousands of loads of fill-dirt to make the enlarged area level with the rest of the temple precincts. It also required a network of roads, bridges, and supporting arches, over an irregular terrain. Access from the south and west was provided for by special stairways and portals. This remarkable engineering feat, which was undertaken by the immensely ambitious Herod, was accomplished about the time of the Savior's ministry.

The Post-Herod Period—Modern Israel

Now we come to the most intriguing part of the story. The temple itself, as will be more fully discussed in a moment, was eventually destroyed by the Romans. In fact, the destruction was so total that even its foundation stones have not yet been discovered, meaning that today no one knows, for sure, exactly where the temple was located. However, the aforementioned massive southern and eastern retaining walls suffered a slightly different fate. Most of them were also eventually destroyed, in part, and were later replaced. However, it is virtually certain that the foundation stones of the present "wailing wall" still date back to the days of King Herod's Temple. These walls are of great importance to us today for the following reason. The present-day orthodox Jews refuse to enter the interior temple precincts for fear of possibly setting foot on the original temple site which, to them, would constitute a heinous sacrilege. As explained, the exact location of this site is unknown, beyond the fact that it lies somewhere inside the enclosed temple precincts. The closest to the actual temple site that orthodox Jews are willing to come, therefore, is the exposed side of the west temple wall originally constructed by Herod. It has become popularly known today as the "Wailing Wall," and it is there that hundreds of thousands of orthodox Jews from all over the world come from time to time to offer their prayers for the return of Israel's glory, and for other appropriate objectives. These prayers and petitions are occasionally inscribed on little pieces of paper which are stuffed into the interstices between the massive stones which compose the wall. You can see them today by the thousands. Non-Jews, as well as Jews who behold this panoramic scene, are moved to tears as they meditate on the tragedies which these long-suffering children of Israel have undergone.

Another little ripple in the stream of history must be considered because its consequences could be of enormous, and even ominous, importance to the entire human race. Islam became a strong military power by the year A.D. 700 (even though Mohammed had only been dead some 70 years), and its suzerainty extended over Jerusalem. One of the Muslims' first undertakings in that city was to construct the celebrated shrine known as the Dome of the Rock. It still stands after thirteen hundred years in shimmering splendor and is easily ranked as the most dazzling architectural work in all of Jerusalem, although far from being the largest. Every Jerusalem cityscape, from whatever angle the city is viewed, is dominated by the large golden dome from which the Dome of the Rock derives its name.

What makes the situation so explosive, however, is that this shrine is located very near, and perhaps even on top of, the site of the temple of Herod, which, in turn, was located on the site of its predecessor temples (Zerubbabel and Solomon). However, the Muslims can legitimately attribute to the site of the Dome of the Rock a special sanctity which equals in every way the sanctity attributed to it by the Jews. The Muslims affirm that it was there that Mohammed, on horseback, ascended to heaven. Guides today point to a depression in a large rock located inside the building, which they believe was caused by Mohammed's horse's hoof as it made that last mighty leap.

This has created a theological impasse of apocalyptic dimensions. The Muslims, who number well over a billion people, are militantly united on matters of showing respect for sacred Islamic sites and icons. The Jews, though tiny in population by comparison, and disparate in their beliefs, are nonetheless equally militantly united in showing reverence for their holy places, and no place on earth is more holy to them than their original temple site.

The built-in ambiguity in this state of affairs results from the fact that the Dome of the Rock was constructed 600 years after the total destruction of the Temple of Herod, and at a time when all traces of the latter had disappeared. The Muslim shrine, as mentioned, may unknowingly have been erected on the temple site itself. No one knows for sure, and since no further exploratory excavations seem to be contemplated, the riddle will presumably never be solved, unless information not now available somehow is miraculously revealed.

Israel's Setting Sun

The last page of our very abbreviated history of the Jewish temple tells the heartbreaking story of the sun's final setting on the glory of Israel and their temple, and of the ensuing desolation of darkness which the Jews were predestined to suffer.

In the year A.D. 70 the Romans made a decision to invade Judea *en masse*. This statement requires a little explanation, however, for in approximately the year 65 B.C. the Romans had already made their first invasion of the Holy Land when the Roman general Pompey entered it with his victorious army. History records that he had the effrontery to force his way, on horseback, right into the Holy of Holies, and noted, with a contemptuous laugh, that this fabled Jewish *sanctum sanctorum* was empty. This was the most scandalous affront that any mortal could have committed, so the Romans got off to a poor start, and it was friction from then on. They exercised suzerainty over Judea up until the final calamity in A.D. 70, but in the meantime allowed the Jews a considerable measure of self-government.

However, Rome's presence was oppressive, and was despised by the Jews, of which fact the New Testament gives abundant proof.

The Jews became increasingly restive, and finally, about forty years after the Savior's resurrection, their intransigence evolved into open rebellion. Faced with this crisis, the reaction of the Romans was: "We've had enough of these Jewish trouble-makers. There is nothing left for us to do but to invade the land in force, and to destroy the last vestiges of opposition. This will serve as an example to the rest of the Empire."

Under general Titus, who later became emperor, a massive expeditionary force was dispatched to this embattled land in A.D. 70. The result of this invasion was the complete demolition of the Jewish nation, which was not recreated until 1948, when modern Israel was reborn. As a result of the Roman conquest, approximately one-third of the Jews were massacred and a large portion sold into slavery. The rest survived the best way they could, many of them interspersing themselves among the various regions of the romanized world.

The most dramatic and visible casualty, however, was the total destruction of the temple which, as we have seen, represented the very life and soul of Jewish religion and culture. Literally not one stone was left standing upon another, thus fulfilling the prediction of the Savior to that effect (see Matt. 24:2).

Temples during the Early Christian Era

A word or two about temples in the early Christian era—did they even exist? The answer is that we have no record of there having been even one. Did the Christians know anything about the temple ordinances as we now know them? We have evidence that they did. One bit of evidence was the occasion when the Savior ascended the Mount of Transfiguration, taking with him Peter, James, and John.

We read of it in the 17th chapter of Matthew. The text does not tell us very much about the event other than that the Savior was transfigured before the three apostles, in the company of Moses and Elijah, who were also transfigured, and that the approving voice of God was heard. That's about all it says. One senses, in reading the account, that there must have transpired much more, about which we are not told. Otherwise, why did Matthew even include the account in his narrative?

However, here's a very slight clue to the reason why the event was so important. On the way down the Savior said that he did not want his three apostles to say anything about what they had seen. "Tell the vision unto no man, until the Son of Man be risen again from the dead" (Matthew 17:9). The belief of the LDS Church is that keys to the sealing power were transferred on the Mount to Peter, James, and John. President Joseph Fielding Smith states:

> Was Elijah reserved to appear in the Kirtland Temple in the Latter-days? What keys did he bestow on Peter, James, and John? Exactly the same keys that he bestowed on the head of Joseph Smith and Oliver Cowdery. . . . The keys that Elijah held were the keys of the everlasting priesthood, the keys of the sealing power which the Lord gave unto him. And that is what he came and bestowed upon the head of Peter, James, and John. And that is what he gave the Prophet Joseph Smith; and that included a ministry of sealing for the living as well as for the dead."[21]

We can presume that Peter, James, and John did communicate to Jesus's other followers, after his resurrection, the details of this remarkable experience and that this information eventually did became common knowledge within the early Christian community. This conclusion is accordant with other evidence supporting the thesis that the early Christians were familiar with the temple ordinances of exaltation.

Let us examine further supporting evidence. There was a 40-day gap between Jesus' resurrection and his ascension into heaven (see Acts 1:3). Every occurrence referred to in the New Testament informing us about what happened during that 40-day gap could have been compressed, timewise, into approximately two days. So that leaves 38 days unaccounted for. Why was there not a single word said about what was happening during that interval of time? After all, out of all the things that Jesus taught his disciples during his three-year ministry, nothing would have excited their curiosity more than a knowledge of the events that occurred during the period between his crucifixion and his resurrection. Why was nothing said about these things?

Again, it is reasonable to surmise that the Savior taught his apostles and intimate disciples the temple ordinances as we understand them. This is consistent with the very fact that we have no word about what was said. Had it been non-confidential material, we would certainly have a record of it. This confidentiality was for the same reason that the Prophet Joseph Smith did not commit to writing, or discuss openly, the details of the temple ordinances as revealed to him.

There is, however, a little wrinkle in this line of reasoning. It might be commented, in passing, that the Savior's visit to the American continent during that period, according to the Book of Mormon account, might account for the silence in the New Testament record. The answer to that commentary would be first, we do not know that the Savior's visit to America occurred during the 40-day period—it most likely took place following it—and, second, even conceding that his visit to America might have occurred during the 40-day period, there would still have been ample time during that same period for Jesus to instruct his disciples in Jerusalem on the sacred temple ordinances.

It is reasonable to conclude that during that 40-day period, or at least part of it, Jesus must have been giving his disciples some very important, but confidential materials, presumably about endowments and eternal sealings.

To further support this conclusion, let me add that within recent times, considerable numbers of ancient documents—codices, scrolls, manuscripts, and books—have been newly discovered, which can be characterized as apocryphal. From a scholar's viewpoint, they are entitled to take their place by the side of the numerous other apocryphal documents which had already been in the possession of scholars for many hundreds of years, some of which date as far back as the earliest Gospel manuscripts themselves. An apocryphal document is one dealing with, or throwing significant light upon, the life and ministry of the Savior but which failed to meet the authenticity tests for canonization imposed by the early Church Fathers. In other words, those ecclesiastical leaders whose authority it was to canonize the scriptures felt that, in the case of the apocrypha, human fantasy had become so intermingled with solid fact that the entire document became suspect, and was therefore rejected on those grounds.

Some of our own LDS scholars have researched these newly discovered apocryphal documents and have found that they, like the others, contain a mixture of materials. Some of them are totally unbelievable and must be rejected. Others, however, are very believable, and need not be totally rejected out of hand. Hence, both LDS and non-LDS scholars now accept the fact that even the apocrypha can throw light upon many of the scriptures' otherwise-unanswered questions. Our own Section 91 in the Doctrine and Covenants confirms the fact that the apocrypha contains both true and false allegations.

Now we come to the point. A number of these apocryphal documents, including both the newly discovered ones, as well as the others, do indeed allege that during the so-called 40-day period the Savior was occupied in teaching his disciples certain secret ordinances and ceremonies. Moreover, additional theological concepts which appear in a number of these documents (including some of the Dead Sea Scrolls) bear a strong resemblance to certain doctrines which we associate with our own temple doctrine. Some of them have to do with the importance and the eternal nature of the marriage covenant and with the actuality of the premortal existence. This latter doctrine has been categorically rejected by other Christian denominations, but unconditionally affirmed by the Latter-day Saints. These allegations show up in sufficiently large numbers and are sufficiently concordant one with the other (and are rendered more believable by the fact that they come from non-collaborating sources), to increase the likelihood that they express certain arcane truths actually taught by the Savior during the 40-day period.

In addition to the above, we also know from 1 Corinthians 15:29 that the early Christians in Corinth practiced baptism for the dead, presumably with Paul's approval. Considering all this evidence, therefore, it is fair to say that the early Christians did have at least some knowledge of our modern temple ordinances of exaltation.

Jewish- and Kirtland-Period Parallels

To conclude this material on the rise and fall of the Jewish temples, let us, for a moment, do an eighteen-hundred-year flash forward. The year is 1838, and the scene is Kirtland, Ohio. Apostasy has shown its ugly face and all is not well with the Kirtland Temple. Bitter arguments have arisen over the question of the temple's ownership and rights of access. Some temple worshippers are showing up wearing pistols and side-arms, for safety's sake. Hatred and mistrust have replaced love and confidence in the hearts of some. The "immovable and unchangeable" brotherhood which the brethren have entered into (see D& C 88:133) has become seriously compromised. Quoting from Elder Boyd K. Packer, "And here [in Kirtland] apostasy took shape and spread with such power as to eventually compel the Prophet to flee to Missouri."[22]

For this reason, the temple soon became "desolate" and had to be abandoned altogether. Although it still stands today, its light has gone out. Though it served its appointed purpose by providing the sacred precincts where the great latter-day work on behalf of he dead could be appropriately inaugurated (see D&C: 110), its other promised blessings were never fully realized. They were conditioned on the Saints' "keeping my [the Lord's] commandments," and on not "polluting this holy house" (D&C 110:8), which conditions apparently were not met.

This troubling sequence of events is just one more confirmation of that well-known adage that "He who refuses to learn the lessons of the past is condemned to relearn them." Fortunately, however, the core of the Church membership remained faithful, and in our subsequent temples received the blessings which circumstances denied them in Kirtland.

3

Temple Symbolism

The Use of Symbols

This chapter discusses the rationale supporting the use of symbols in the temple ordinances. In the first chapter the endowment patron emerges from his first temple experience a bit glassy eyed from sheer bewilderment, because the temple ceremony is so overpowering and contains so many symbols that fall outside the context of his religious experience. We note, for example, in a typical Latter-day Saint chapel there are no symbols to be found whatsoever, other than the sacramental emblems—no crosses or crucifixes, no images or pictures, no vestments, no altars—nothing. To the novice, the temple ceremony, heavily interspersed with symbols, can prove disconcerting. His bewilderment is understandable.

However, those with even a superficial knowledge of the scriptures well know that the latter have frequently used symbols to teach and reenforce moral lessons. Since symbols are appropriate for use in scriptures, it should come as no surprise that they are considered appropriate for temple ordinances as well, inasmuch as the latter are only another form of scripture.

Elder John A. Widtsoe, in his book, *Temple Worship,* and quoted by Boyd K. Packer in *The Holy Temple,* says: "We live in a world of symbols. No man or woman can come out of the temple endowed as he should be, unless he has seen, beyond the symbol, the mighty realities for which the symbols stand."

Let me pursue the use of symbols in sacred scripture a little further. Let's take the book of Isaiah as an example. When was the last time you relaxed in a nice comfortable chair and spent the evening reading this great book *for pure enjoyment?* The answer is, *never.* Why? Because you don't understand it—it's as simple as that. For that reason, any spontaneous joy you might otherwise have derived from the book is dead on arrival. This statement is not intended as criticism of this amazing book, for Isaiah was clearly the most important of all the Old Testament prophets. The Lord told the Nephites that "Great are the words of Isaiah" (3 Ne. 23:1-3), and the latter is quoted more in the Book of Mormon and the Doctrine and Covenants than any other prophet. The statement is simply one of fact. Portions of the book are unintelligible to the novice because of their heavy use of symbols and because of the apparent absence of a key to make them understandable.

I remember hearing a General Authority, somewhat humorously, make the comment that many conscientious Church members start out reading the Book of Mormon with stiffened jaw, determined to continue their pursuit right through to the very end. Everything goes well until they reach the twentieth chapter of First Nephi, which begins the Isaiah passages. At that point, Isaiah becomes their acid test of survivorship, and many of them bail out right there. Those who pass the test continue on bravely to the end, but later confess that, looking back, they didn't get very much out of Isaiah, and that it was pure will-power that pulled them through.

In support of my statement that the Book of Isaiah is difficult, and in some cases impossible to understand, I offer the following passage as my exhibit A:

> Doth the plowman plow all day to sow? doth he open and break the clods of his ground? when he hath made plain the face thereof, doth he not cast abroad the fitches and scatter the cummin and cast in the principal wheat and the appointed barley and the rye in their place? For his God doth instruct him to discretion and doth teach him. For the fitches are not threshed with a threshing instrument, neither is a cart wheel turned about upon the cummin; but the fitches are beaten out with a staff, and the cummin with the rod. Bread corn is bruised; because he will not ever be threshing it, nor break it with the wheel of his cart, nor bruise it with his horseman (Isaiah 28:24-28).[23]

Now, I invite you to fathom the real meaning of this strangely worded passage. Even if you are told that fitches and cumin are vegetables related to the carrot family and known for their aromatic seeds, you will still have to confess complete bewilderment.

Many of us today take satisfaction in being able to say: "I never beat about the bush, but call a spade a spade." This is typical red-blooded Americana: a proud carryover from the spirit of the robust American frontier. Yet the plain fact of the matter is that Isaiah is beating about the bush and he is not calling a spade a spade. Let's be honest and admit it. We sometimes suppose that talking this frankly about a prophet of the Lord is disrespectful or that taking his rhetorical symbolism literally is a praiseworthy exhibition of religious orthodoxy. The truth is that recognizing that the prophets of old frequently talked in symbols is simply accepting an indisputable reality. The sooner we recognize this fact, the sooner we will understand what they were talking about. In interpreting scripture, the Lord expects us to use both our faith and our common sense.

In the above-cited passage, Isaiah seemed on the surface to be talking about fitches and cumin. But he wasn't really talking about them at all. Nor was he writing a handbook on Jewish farming practices. What he was really talking about was the fate of Israel. According to one interpretation (although there may be many), his message was that Israel was like hard stubborn soil which first had to be broken up with a plow to make ready for the planting of the fitches and cumin, which Latter-day Saints might envision as possibly referring to the restoration of the gospel. This plowing and breaking up of the hard clods involves arduous work and much suffering. In other words, Isaiah told the Israelites that they were in for hard times.

But the story doesn't end there. Israel then symbolically becomes the fitches and cumin. Having endured their martyrdom and having subsequently accepted the Messianic message, penitent Israel is now "harvested" and prepared for threshing, and processing (i.e., receiving her final judgment). But the punishment must fit the crime. Just as a farmer does not use the same methods for threshing or processing soft and fragile crops, such as fitches and cumin, as he does for hard crops, such as wheat and barley, so God will temper his punishment to Israel and will take into account the promises he has made to her and the suffering she had been called on to endure.

Admittedly, a little imagination is required to fathom the above interpretation, but it makes sense, and is consistent with Isaiah's major prophetic theme which runs throughout his book, namely the final redemption of Israel. In other words, Isaiah tells us that the story of Israel has a happy ending. Of one thing we may be absolutely certain, and that is that the reader is not supposed to take Isaiah's references to fitches and cumin literally.

We are still left with the unanswered question: if Isaiah is talking about Israel, why doesn't he say so? Why does he talk about fitches and cumin instead? Why all these rhetorical acrobatics? And why doesn't he even give us a clue? Why is he playing games with us?

The same question might be asked about the temple ceremonies. Much of it is symbolic, and we are not always certain what lies behind the symbol. Why this circuitous route to the celestial kingdom when a straight one would do just as well?

Explaining the Use of Symbols

The robust "call-a-spade-a-spade" American frontiersman will just have to be patient and try to understand the reasons for the use of symbols. I shall first briefly present two less important, but still perfectly valid, reasons for the use of symbolism in the scriptures, and they will be followed by a much more important reason, which requires a more extended explanation.

The first reason, or explanation, is that for much of its early history Israel was a subjugated nation, having been conquered or politically dominated successively by the Egyptians, the Assyrians, the Babylonians, the Persians, the Greeks, and the Romans. Subjugated people have a tendency to develop code words to replace literal words whose use might get them into trouble.

For example, when the Savior said, "Whosoever shall compel thee to go a mile, go with him twain" (Matthew 5:41), he was using code words, and everyone knew it. The Roman law required any able-bodied Jew to obey a Roman soldier's order to assist him in carrying his baggage for one mile. The Savior, in teaching us that we should go even beyond what was required as a token of our willingness to establish loving relationships with our fellow men, was using the symbolism of this much-hated Roman law to make his point even stronger. Yet he did it without even mentioning the Romans.

A second explanation for scriptural symbolism is that Semitic languages, including Hebrew, lend themselves very easily to poetic, and therefore figurative expression. They are more adaptable to the use of symbols than are the Western-European languages, which are more matter-of-fact. The latter characteristic is good for science, but not as good for poetry.

But now we come to what I consider to be the more important reasons why the Lord has given us so much of his message in symbols. This reason applies today, as much as it did in days of yore. To put the explanation in context, let me refer, first of all, to section 84 of the Doctrine and Covenants. There we read:

> Now this Moses plainly taught to the children of Israel in the wilderness, and sought diligently to sanctify his people that they might behold the face of God; but they hardened their hearts and could not endure his presence; therefore, the Lord in his wrath, . . . swore that they should not enter into his rest while in the wilderness, which rest is the fulness of his glory. Therefore, he took Moses out of their midst, and the Holy Priesthood also; and the lesser priesthood continued, which priesthood holdeth the key of the ministering of angels and the preparatory gospel . . . (D&C 84:23-26).

Because of Israel's disobedience, it forfeited the right to receive and retain the higher, or Melchizedek priesthood, which holds the "key of the mysteries of the kingdom, even the key of the knowledge of God" (v. 19). Instead of that, they were allowed to retain the Aaronic Priesthood and were given the Law of Moses, which was to foreshadow the advent of the Messiah, in preparation for receiving the higher law.

At that point, the picture becomes a little complicated. For the following 1,400 years, the religious practices of the Israelites were in the hands of the Levitical and Aaronic priesthoods, who administered the numerous blood sacrifices and other rituals in compliance with the requirements of the Mosaic law. As mentioned, these sacrifices acted as a type and shadow, prefiguring the actual sacrificial atonement of their Messiah, Jesus Christ. This fact is confirmed in modern scripture (Moses 5:7).

However, it is doubtful whether most of those involved in these elaborate preparatory ordinances fully understood for what purpose they were intended. It is one of history's greatest ironies that when the glorious event for which they had been preparing themselves for 1,400 years finally arrived, Israel, as a corporate religious body, failed either to identify it for what it was or to comprehend its significance. Though the law was to have acted as a schoolmaster to lead Israel to Christ (Gal. 3:24), when he finally arrived they "received not our [his] witness" (John 3:11) and thus condemned themselves to a long night of darkness and estrangement.

That only tells half the story. The other half is that God did not want the knowledge of the Messiah's coming, nor of the Atonement, nor the role of the Melchizedek Priesthood, to be entirely obliterated from the earth during this 1,400-year hiatus. Accepting the fact that the corporate religious body, Israel, was not yet ready to receive this information, as we learned above, the fact remained that there were always some—the few out of many—who were. These were the prophets of the Old Testament. They held the Melchizedek Priesthood and testified of the coming of the Messiah. In fact, the Book of Mormon makes it plain that every authentic prophet of God did so testify, because that is one of the callings of a real prophet. "For behold, did not Moses prophesy unto them concerning the coming of the Messiah, and that God should redeem his people? Yea, and even all the prophets who had prophesied since the world began—have they not spoken more or less concerning these things?" (Mosiah 13:33).

Among those prophets who testified of the coming of the Messiah were included, *a fortiori,* a number of Book of Mormon prophets, since the principal mission of the Book of Mormon was and is to act as a special witness of the divine mission of our Savior Jesus Christ. For example, the Book of Mormon's title page reads: ". . . and also to the convincing of the Jew and Gentile that Jesus is the Christ, the eternal God, manifesting himself unto all Nations." We are reassured in the Book of Mormon that there were some during that intermediate period who were filled with the spirit of prophecy, and who well understood Isaiah's prophecies about the coming of the the Messiah, even though others (the vast majority) rejected his predictions as being too hard to understand: ". . . for because the words of Isaiah are not plain unto you, nevertheless they are plain unto all those that are filled with the spirit of prophecy" (see 2 Ne. 25:4).

It must be noted, however, that the Old Testament prophetic references to the Messiah are, for the most part, expressed in veiled, or highly symbolic, rhetoric. A few of them, however, are less veiled. The references to Christ in chapter 53 of Isaiah, and especially verses 3-9, are probably the most well-known. Latter-day Saints cannot entertain the slightest doubt whatsoever as to the one about whom Isaiah was speaking. Yet it is always surprising to learn that many men and women who have devoted most of their adult lives to the study of the Old Testament do not agree with our interpretation.

Two questions immediately come to mind. First, why did the Lord see fit to place in the holy scriptures so many prophetic references to the coming of the Messiah, in view of the fact that those for whom they were primarily intended, namely the House of Israel, didn't believe them, which fact the Lord knew in advance? And, second, why did he inspire his prophets to clothe their messianic prophecies in such veiled language?

Regarding the first question, it can appropriately be pointed out that even though these Old Testament messianic passages had little effect on the Jews themselves, they greatly inspired and strengthened the faith of subsequent Christians down through the years. They looked back, in retrospect, and saw to what extent these prophecies were fulfilled by the advent of the Messiah in the meridian of times. Through them, Christian faith has been marvelously strengthened, and the world made better. Handel's *Messiah,* as a specific example, has probably brought more inspiration to more people than has any other piece of music ever composed. Those familiar with its lyrics understand to what extent Handel drew inspiration from Old Testament messianic predictions in creating his immortal musical masterpiece. And so it is with countless other composers, painters, sculptors, poets, and artists of every category.

It can also be argued that these numerous Old Testament prophetic references to the coming of the Messiah laid the foundation for the restoration of the gospel in modern times.

Other reasons may occur to the reader, as they do to me, but without further pursuing the point, I shall move on to the second question raised above. Why is so much scriptural material, especially in the Old Testament, and also, to a lesser degree, in the modern temple ordinances, expressed in difficult-to-understand, symbolic language?

From a careful examination of Old Testament scriptures, it can be fairly deduced that Old Testament revelations from God came to the children of Israel on two different levels of understanding. On the one hand was the lower-level message, intended for those on the level of the Law of Moses. Then there was the higher level, or "gospel-level" message, intended for those (presumably a small minority) who were already prepared to receive it. What is significant is that the Lord saw fit to formulate his two messages (one for those on the lower level, and the other, for those on the higher level) *within one and the same text.* This is the key.

For those on the Law-of-Moses level, the language was clear and understandable. It dealt essentially with obedience to the Law of Moses, with Israel's need for repentance, and with prophesies concerning Israel's future destiny. For those messages on the higher, or gospel level dealing with the Messiah's coming and mission, the language was more symbolic, or, as we would say, today, "encoded." The two types of language thus became intermingled in the same text, and each category of recipients read into the text the message intended for it.

The Lord's alternative to the above arrangement would have been to separate the material according to the level of understanding of its recipients, and to compose two entirely different texts, one containing the higher level material (but in clear and unambiguous language) and the other containing the lower level material. But that would have left the higher, or gospel-level material also exposed to those on the lower level, whom the Lord had apparently decided were not yet ready to receive it.

The solution was to combine both messages into one text, the higher message being encoded, but intelligible to those operating on the higher frequency, but unintelligible to those operating on the lower frequency. If there is any mystery about this, recall that during World War II, countless messages were exchanged among allies containing both a straightforward message on the one hand, but also, embodied within them there were encoded messages intended for the underground whose lives would have been forfeited if the hidden message had been first decoded by the enemy. The message on the higher level, being expressed more symbolically, is more susceptible to being added upon by the Lord at a later date, whereas the message on the lower level, being more specific, is not.

A second reason for the ambiguity of language, quite different from the first, might be that if the Lord had made his messianic message too specific, his children might have less need to exercise their agency in developing faith in the Messiah. "There are so many things that he [God] could do to rend the veil. But 'we walk by faith, not by sight' (2 Cor. 5:7). . . . God has chosen to leave us free, amid circumstances that do not compel belief. . . ."[24]

The Lord apparently inspired the prophets of Israel to embody in their one prophetic text a message for both those who were not yet ready to receive the higher message, and those who were. Both could read the same text and draw from it the message which their level of spirituality qualified them to receive. Thus, those of greater spirituality could read Isaiah and receive a spiritual witness that he was referring to the redemptive role of the coming Messiah, whereas those of less spiritual enlightenment could read the same text and draw therefrom a lesser, but nevertheless valuable message.

This "double meaning" pattern is nothing unique to Isaiah, but has been carefully followed, again and again, in the formulation of scriptural texts. The best known example of this was given by the Savior himself. We all remember his parable of the sower who went forth to sow. His seed fell on four different types of ground. The first was so rocky that it failed to take root at all. The second had such shallow soil that although the seed did take root, the seedlings very quickly withered and died. The third produced good growth but was quickly choked by competing thorns and weeds. The fourth eventually produced a bounteous harvest.

After giving the parable, the Savior's disciples came to him and asked, in effect, the very same question that we are now considering:

Why did you make your parable so difficult to understand? Please be kind enough to explain to us what you were really saying.

The Savior then patiently explained to them that he had intentionally been talking *on two different levels of understanding*. On the one level is a story of interest to farmers. On a higher level is a spiritual message dealing with human receptivity to the gospel message.

Listen to his words: ". . . because it is given unto you to know the mysteries of the kingdom of heaven, but to them it is not given. . . . Therefore, speak I to them in parables: because they seeing see not; and hearing they hear not, neither do they understand." (Matt. 13:10-11, 13).

On another occasion, Jesus told his disciples "Whoso eateth my flesh, and drinketh my blood, hath eternal life; and I will raise him up at the last day" (John 6:54). This statement was not only religiously unacceptable, but culturally repulsive to most of this followers, who had been brought up to believe that drinking any kind of blood, or eating any non-kosher food, was absolute anathema. As a result, he lost his crowd and caused even his closest associates to begin to wonder. They were taking his allegory literally, instead of symbolically, and to them it didn't make any sense. They were still at the lower level of understanding; he was on the higher.

There is still another reason why the Lord sometimes speaks to us in hard-to-understand symbols. This question seems to presume that knowledge is always preferable to ignorance. But that may not always be correct. Celestial knowledge is like a fire: the inexperienced who handle it may get burned. As was explained in chapter one, the scriptures are replete with statements to the effect that those with greater knowledge must carry a greater responsibility.

In modern scripture a certain theme runs like a thread throughout, namely that a special responsibility is placed on those who receive special blessings. "For of him unto whom much is given, much is required; and he who sins against the greater light shall receive the greater condemnation" (D&C 82:3).

Frightening are the implications of 2 Peter 2:20-21, and 2 Ne. 31:14, wherein we are told that it would be far better for us never to have received the truth than to receive it and then reject it.

In view of God's full knowledge of our own weaknesses and our unpreparedness to receive the greater light, who are we to say that he is not doing us a service, rather than a disservice, by withholding certain knowledge until we are more ready to receive it?

Why is so much of the temple message conveyed to us in symbols? The answer seems to be straightforward. The Lord desires all Latter-day Saints to receive their temple ordinances of exaltation, regardless of their level of understanding, provided that they are worthy. These ordinances are the gate through which all must eventually pass. But these ordinances are not simple, and are not supposed to be simple. After all, they embrace all of life and plumb the depths of eternity. Human mortals cannot understand everything that God eventually wants them to know.

He gives us a portion of this celestial knowledge in the form of symbols, well knowing that we will not understand their entire meaning, but will understand *as much of it as our level of spiritual enlightenment permits*. We clearly understand the covenants we enter into regarding the commitments the Lord wants us to make. There is no ambiguity there. Beyond that, we are left in an open-ended situation; as our spiritual understanding enlarges, our understanding of the temple ordinances will also enlarge. Symbolic language lends itself more easily to subsequent enlargement than does specific language. Thus, the total temple experience should be a lifetime one, with each individual visit bringing with it new understandings and fresh insights. It must never end.

Perhaps it might be appropriate to mention a few temple symbols which are well known and which do not involve any confidentiality.

1. ***Use of (consecrated) oil.*** Because olive oil is so pure, it has always been used for ceremonial purposes as a symbol of moral purity. Originally, olive oil was a source of both heat and light. It was both food for nourishment and medicine for internal intake. It was also a balm for external application to wounds. Little wonder, then, that the olive tree was the most venerated tree in Israel.

2. ***Reason for (most) LDS temples to face east.*** Symbolizes the fact that we are anxiously awaiting the Lord's return to earth from the east (see Matt. 24:27).

3. ***Use of the three-spire motif in the Salt Lake temple (and others).*** Symbolic of the threefold nature of the Godhead.

4. ***Wearing of white and uniform vestments for all who perform ordinances in the temple.*** Symbolize purity and holiness and symbolize the equality of all before the Lord.

5. ***Locating the baptismal font in the lowest part of the temple,*** symbolizing the rising of the dead from their graves (D&C 128:12-13).

6. ***Baptismal fonts are always positioned on the backs of twelve oxen,*** presumably symbolic of the twelve tribes of Israel (1 Kgs. 7:25).

There are many more.

The reader is referred to Matthew B. Brown's, and Paul Thomas Smith's *Symbols in Stone,* and to Allen H. Barber's *Celestial Symbols—Symbolism in Doctrine, Religious Traditions and Temple Architecture.*[25] I close this chapter with a quotation from Elder Joseph Fielding McConkie:

> Symbols are the timeless and universal language in which God, in his wisdom, has chosen to teach this gospel and bear witness of his Son. They are the language of the scriptures, the language of revelation, the language of the Spirit, the language of faith. Symbols are the language common to the saints in all generations. Symbols are the language in which all gospel covenants and ordinances of salvation have been revealed. They are a means whereby we enrich, deepen, and enhance understanding and expression. They enable us to give visual and conceptual form to ideas and feeling that may otherwise defy the power of word. Symbols take us beyond the language of words, granting us an eloquence in the expression of feelings. . . . To be literate in the things of the Spirit is to be fluent in the language of symbols.[26]

4
The Ecstasy and the Agony

The distinguished writer Irving Stone once wrote a biography of Michelangelo entitled "The Agony and the Ecstasy." A fitting title for the Kirtland chapter of the Mormon odyssey could be composed by simply transposing those two words into "The Ecstasy and the Agony." During that period the Saints reached spiritual heights equal to anything recorded in ancient times. But then night followed day, as it always does. The Saints' experiences became so disappointing that only the strong could hold on long enough to reach the next cycle of ecstasy and agony, which was soon to follow.

In tracing the development of the modern-day temple, we'll start with the ecstasy of the Kirtland period (1831-1838), during which the foundations were laid for all that followed, continuing even to the present day. Seventy-seven canonized revelations were received from the Lord during that brief six-year period, which were well over half of all those received since the first day of the Restoration until now. In fact, sixty-three canonized revelations were received within the space of three-years. The Prophet's age during that brief period ranged from 25 to 28.

During the period we are considering, the Saints developed a special revelatory relationship with the Lord that seems to have been historically unique. During this same period the first modern-day temple appeared, although, curiously, the word "temple" never appears in the Doctrine and Covenants in its connection. That is *our* term. In the Doctrine and Covenants it is simply called the "House of the Lord." The word "temple" is used several times in connection with the two abortive Missouri temples and the Nauvoo temple, but never in connection with the one in Kirtland. The reason, perhaps, is that the latter was a multi-purpose building, including those purposes served by our present-day chapels as well as the performance of sacred ordinances and the receiving of revelations. The temple ordinances as we now know them were not known until the Nauvoo period, although in Kirtland we find their beginnings.

The Exodus to Kirtland

In search of an explanation for the exodus of the Church from New York to Kirtland, Ohio, in early 1831, we can appropriately begin our story with Parley P. Pratt, a man whose later influence on the Church was monumental. In the late 1820's, he emigrated from upstate New York to a small community just west of Cleveland, Ohio. It so happened that one Sidney Rigdon, the pastor of a Disciples of Christ congregation located in the tiny community of Mentor, just east of Cleveland, and just a stone's throw from Kirtland, was visiting the area where Parley P. Pratt had settled, to do some proselytizing for his own faith. Rigdon was persuasive and soon met and converted Pratt. The latter's strong religious instincts caused him to return to New York as a missionary for his newly found faith.

So when he reached the general area of Fayette, New York, the inevitable happened: a copy of the Book of Mormon fell into his hands. One of the Church's most faith-promoting stories deals with his reaction to this marvelous book, which had just come off the press. After devouring its contents on the spot he became a thrall to its overpowering message. He forthwith jettisoned his affiliation with the Disciples of Christ and traveled to Palmyra to meet the Prophet Joseph Smith. There he was baptized into what was soon to be officially named The Church of Jesus Christ of Latter-day Saints, and was ordained an elder. His miraculous conversion has been made the subject of a well-known film with which many Latter-day Saints are familiar.

Soon thereafter, the Prophet sent a group of four elders on a proselytizing assignment which was to carry them to the state of Missouri, and thence to the Lamanite tribes across the Missouri River. Parley P. Pratt, Oliver Cowdery, Peter Whitmer, and Ziba Peterson were the four selected to undertake this arduous and risky venture.

As we reconstruct what happened as they took their departure, Brother Pratt must have said to his three companions something like this: "While we are on our way to the western frontier, why don't we stop off at my old home territory, to see whether we might make some converts there. Specifically, let's go to Mentor, where my good friend Pastor Sidney Rigdon resides, and also to Kirtland, which is close by, and where he has a sizeable congregation."

No sooner it was said than done. The group did arrive in Mentor, and Elder Pratt did contact Sidney Rigdon. The tables were then turned: the former converted now became the converter, and vice versa. Rigdon read the Book of Mormon. Though skeptical at first, he finally accepted its message, and the reality of the Restoration, and was baptized. This was a pivotal event for the Church, for Rigdon not only subsequently converted a large number of his Disciples of Christ flock to his newly found faith, but in his own right became perhaps the Church's most eloquent preacher and served as first counselor to the Prophet for twelve years during the Church's infancy.

The immediate cause for the Church's removal to Kirtland grew out of the difficulties the Prophet encountered while translating the Bible in Fayette, New York. This was late in 1830, after Brother Pratt and his associates had already departed on their mission. The opposition to the Prophet became so unendurably intense that it was impossible for him to continue his work. It was by revelation, therefore, that he and the early converts were instructed to assemble in Ohio (see D&C 37:3). This transfer of venue was almost inevitable because they couldn't remain in New York, and a ready-made congregation was awaiting them in Kirtland. That congregation formed a stable nucleus around which the Church could rapidly expand its numbers. Acting by inspiration, the Church, and most of the members, including the Prophet and his family, migrated to Kirtland.

The story of his arrival there is a familiar one. It was early in February of 1831, and the snow was deep. The Prophet and his wife Emma drew up in a sleigh to the Gilbert & Whitney general store. The Prophet promptly jumped out, walked briskly into the store, and confronted Newel K. Whitney, one of the proprietors. Extending his hand he said, "Newel K.Whitney, thou art the man." The latter responded, "You have the better of me, sir. I could not have identified you as you have identified me," or words to that effect. The Prophet then answered: "I am the Prophet Joseph Smith. You have prayed me here. Now what do you want?"

It so happened that Newel K. Whitney and his wife had recently joined the Church through the efforts of Sidney Rigdon, but still had a number of unanswered questions on their minds. This was quite natural. As a result, they had frequently gone to the Lord, on their knees, seeking confirmation of their decision to join and pleading for someone to come and give them further enlightenment. And so the Prophet, by his astonishing response to Brother Whitney's supplication and by his subsequent explanations, gave Brother Whitney and his wife the reassurance they were looking for. Their prayers had been fully answered.

This little vignette turned out to be of unbelievably historic significance, first, because Brother Whitney became one of the Church's most stalwart members, remaining true to it to the end of his life and serving as Presiding Bishop for three years; and, second, because he provided the Prophet and his wife with a place in which to live, which, under the circumstances, couldn't have been more needed had it come to them as manna from heaven.

Early Revelations and Miracles; the Temple Foreseen

So Joseph and Emma lived, intermittently, during much of the Kirtland period, in the upstairs residential section of the Whitney store. This is of particular importance, for it was in the room adjacent to their bedroom that many of the Prophet's most important revelations were received, including sections 88, 89, and, 93, to mention just three. It was also there that the School of the Prophets held many of its meetings.

During their approximately four-year period of residence in the Whitney home, the Prophet and Emma were obliged to temporarily remove to Hiram, Ohio, located approximately 30 miles from Kirtland, where they stayed in the home of "Father" John Johnson. The reasons for this removal were the same as those which had forced them to remove to Kirtland in the first place: interference and opposition by the Church's adversaries. Ironically, in Hiram they soon encountered the same kind of diabolical opposition, requiring them eventually to move back to Kirtland.

It was in Hiram that seventeen canonized revelations were received by the Prophet, including the most celebrated of them all, namely Section 76 of the Doctrine and Covenants, of which we shall say more later. It was also during the Prophet's Hiram residency that that infamous incident occurred in which an infuriated mob dragged him by the heels out of bed and thence outdoors into sub-freezing winter weather.

Several of his assailants voted for his assassination, but they finally settled on tarring and feathering him.

Returning to Kirtland, it is of interest that the Whitney store not only is still standing, but has been restored to its pristine state. In fact, it won a national award for being one of the finest and most authentic restorations in the nation, *à la* Williamsburg. It is a "must" for visitors to Kirtland to see, in addition to the temple itself.

Of far greater importance to the spiritually inquisitive visitor than a visit to the store itself, however, is a visit to the Prophet's above-mentioned second-floor living quarters and to his adjacent sanctuary reserved for receiving revelations. No one can enter the latter without recalling the words revealed to the Prophet in that very room: ". . . my glory shall be there, and my presence shall be there" (D&C 94:8).

Of particular interest to our discussion on temples is the aforesaid section 88 of the Doctrine and Covenants, also revealed to the Prophet in that same room. In that revelation the reference to a temple (therein called a "house of God") was the first of a series of revelations which would increase our understanding of the reason for temples and of their association with what we now call "work for the dead." Every temple subsequently built can view itself as a symbolic offspring of that famous section 88.

Let us discuss this section for a moment, for it is crucial to our understanding of all that was to follow. It deals with a multitude of subjects—at least 15—but we shall refer to only two. In verse 127, the Saints are instructed to prepare a "school of the prophets."

Earlier, in verse 119, the Saints are told to: "Organize yourselves; prepare every needful thing; and establish a house, even a house of prayer, a house of fasting, a house of faith, a house of learning, a house of glory, a house of order, and a house of God . . ."

The above two verses involve two distinctly different instructions: the first, to establish a School of the Prophets, and the second, to establish a House of God (i.e., to build a temple). This seems to be clear, and the verses have generally been so interpreted. Based upon that interpretation, the Saints did, in fact, proceed to establish a School of the Prophets and to construct a temple, as instructed. The latter, however, was delayed somewhat.

The school of the prophets is brought into the picture in our narrative because there existed historical links between it and the proposed temple. The prescribed standards of comportment prescribed for participation in the School of the Prophets became the model, when the time came, to formulate standards of comportment for participation in the soon-to-be-revealed temple ordinances.

These standards of comportment applicable to the School of the Prophets are set forth in D&C 88, starting with verse 128. Among other things, it was stipulated that he who was appointed to be president or teacher of the group was to exchange salutations of eternal love with the other members, which involved uplifting his hands to heaven, and saluting the brother, or brothers, with the words "Art thou a brother (or brethren)? I salute you in the name of the Lord Jesus Christ, in token or remembrance of the everlasting covenant, in which covenant I receive you to fellowship, in a determination that is fixed, immovable, and unchangeable, to be your friend and brother through the grace of God in the bonds of love, to walk in all the commandments of God blameless, in thanksgiving forever and ever, amen" (D&C 88:133).

The rules of conduct applicable to present-day temples are not as specifically formalized as were the above, but they embody the same underlying principle, namely: there must be no contention or disputation in the temple of the Lord. The law of the temple, as was the law of the School of the Prophets, is the law of love, and those whose hearts are filled with rancor or retribution should wait until those unholy feelings have passed them by before entering the Lord's most holy place.

> . . . he that hath the spirit of contention is not of me, but is of the devil, who is the father of contention, and he stirreth up the hearts of men to contend with anger, one with another. Behold, this is not my doctrine, to stir up the hearts of men with anger, one against another; but this is my doctrine, that such things should be done away (3 Ne. 11:29-30).

The instruction in verse 70 "to call a solemn assembly" probably refers both to the formation of the School of the Prophets, which instruction was carried out almost immediately, and also to the conducting of the solemn assembly associated with the dedication of the temple, which occurred approximately four years later. This was confirmed in the dedicatory prayer of the Kirtland Temple (see D&C 109:6).

Before telling more of the story of the construction and dedication of the Kirtland Temple, it would be appropriate to first relate a few incidents occurring in Kirtland during the pre-temple period, which support our characterizing it as one of ecstasy.

Brother Karl Ricks Anderson, an acknowledged authority on the Kirtland period, in his book entitled *Joseph Smith's Kirtland, Eyewitness Accounts* states:

> The visions and appearances of Deity [i.e. both the Father and the Son] in the Kirtland area that have been documented, number at least into the teens and took place at four separate sites. Several witnesses also included descriptions of heavenly beings.
>
> Joseph Smith, Lyman Wight, and Harvey Whitlock received a vision of both God the Father and his Son Jesus Christ, in the log schoolhouse on the Isaac Morley farm, during a conference held from June 3 to 6, 1831. Levi Hancock recorded that the Prophet was speaking to the elders, when he stepped out on the floor and said: 'I now see God, and Jesus Christ at his right hand. Let them kill me, I should not feel death as I am now.[27]

In *An Early Latter-day Saint History: The Book of John Whitmer*, we read the following entry by John Whitmer, the official Church historian and recorder, regarding the above meeting:

> The Spirit of the Lord fell upon Joseph in an unusual manner. . . . After he had prophesied he laid his hands upon Lyman Wight [and ordained him] to the High Priesthood. . . . and the Spirit fell upon Lyman, and he prophesied, concerning the coming of Christ. . . . he saw the heavens opened, and the Son of Man sitting on the right hand of the Father. Making intercession for his brethren, the Saints. He said that God would work a work in these last days that tongue cannot express, and the mind is not capable to conceive. The glory of the Lord shone around.[28]

I am reporting here three episodes, out of many more, in which other persons in addition to the Prophet saw the Father and the Son during this narrow window of time (1831-1833). The first is the meeting reported above. The second episode was the one resulting in the revelation now known as Section 76 of the Doctrine and Covenants, dealing with the three degrees of glory. This revelation is, perhaps, the greatest of them all. The site was not the Whitney store in Kirtland, but, as previously mentioned, an upstairs room in the home of John Johnson in Hiram, Ohio. Today, visitors can enter that very room where this historic revelation was given, and can envision with rapturous delight, the events which occurred there many years ago.

By way of historical background, the headnotes to Section 76 of the Doctrine and Covenants read as follows:

> A vision given to Joseph Smith the Prophet and Sidney Rigdon at Hiram, Ohio, February 16, 1832. HC 1:245-252. Prefacing his record of this vision the Prophet wrote: "Upon my return from Amherst conference, I resumed the translation of the Scriptures. From sundry revelations which had been received, it was apparent that many important points touching the salvation of man had been taken from the Bible, or lost before it was compiled. It appeared self-evident from what truths were left, that if God rewarded everyone according to the deeds done in the body, the term 'Heaven,' as intended for the Saints' eternal home, must include more kingdoms than one. Accordingly, while translating St. John's Gospel, myself and Elder Rigdon saw the following vision." It was after the Prophet had translated John 5:29 that this vision was given.

This vision confirmed the validity of Joseph's surmise and gave to the world the details of man's ultimate destiny and the three degrees of heavenly glory, to one of which each one of us is ultimately destined to go. The mere reading of these majestic verses causes one's heart to throb with excitement.

On this occasion a number of brethren, perhaps ten or twelve, had assembled in this small room, including the Prophet Joseph Smith and Sidney Rigdon, who had been acting as his scribes. Prayer had been offered petitioning the Lord for further light on the nature of mankind's resurrection and eventual exaltation.

Suddenly, the answer came in a burst of glory. It was the Prophet and Sidney Rigdon alone who were privy to its message. The others could only sit and wait. This terrifyingly powerful revelation came rolling in from afar, impacting like a tidal wave from eternity upon the astonished

Prophet and his companion. It brought with it a clear understanding of the glories and mysteries of God's creation and of the ultimate destiny of mankind. It was a celestial experience, almost without parallel. In their rapture, these two men sat immobile and transfixed by what they were seeing and hearing. Their silence was broken only by an occasional: "Do you see what I see?" which question was answered by a "Yes, and do you see what I see?"

This continued for about an hour, when the vision finally dissolved. We are told that after it was over, Sidney Rigdon turned wobbly and pale from sheer exhaustion. The Prophet, however, still as strong as a lion, smiled and commented: "Sidney isn't as used to this as I am." This was one of those famous little snippets of humor appearing in a profoundly serious context, throwing light on the Prophet's amazingly complex but delightful personality.

Joseph, aided by his companion, very quickly and meticulously recorded what the two of them had seen and heard. In the text of the revelation, we have, among other things, one of the most splendid declarations, or testimonies, of the living reality of the Savior of mankind to be found anywhere in the world. One wonders on what basis the claim can be made that Latter-day Saints are not Christians. We can only wish that the entire world would read the Prophet's testimony. Here are his words:

> And now, after the many testimonies which have been given of him, this is the testimony, last of all, which we give of him: That he lives! For we saw him, even on the right hand of God; and we heard the voice bearing record that he is the Only Begotten of the Father—That by him, and through him, and of him, the worlds are and were created, and the inhabitants thereof are begotten sons and daughters unto God (D&C 76:22-24).

To read that testimony recalls to mind the Lord's instruction given elsewhere: "Trifle not with sacred things" (D&C 6:12). The above passage is too sacred to trifle with. It must be read in soberness and will command the respect of every fair-minded man or woman who reads it.

Two further points might appropriately be made. First is the fact that the revelation consumed about an hour in the giving, and yet the account of it in the Doctrine and Covenants can be carefully read in ten minutes. It would appear that the bulk of their revelation was not reduced to writing. Why was it not? We are given the answer, right within the body of the revelation itself. It says: "But great and marvelous are the works of the Lord, and the mysteries of his kingdom . . . which surpass all understanding in glory, and in might, and in dominion. . . . and are not lawful for man to utter (vv.114-115).

That makes sense. These are celestial experiences. How does one express a celestial experience in an earthly vocabulary? One has only to study almost any foreign language to understand how impossible it is to translate into English some of that language's idiomatic expressions for which there is no English equivalent. He would understand the impossibility of bringing heavenly thoughts down to earth and clothing them in earthly habiliments.

What we are given in Section 76, wonderfully lucid though it may be in explaining man's ultimate destiny, seems to offer us no more than a small portion of all that is knowable on this subject. For the rest, we shall have to wait. "Ye are not able to abide the presence of God now, neither the ministering of angels; wherefore, continue in patience until ye are perfected" (D&C 67:13).

The second commentary might also be made that the circumstances surrounding the receiving of the revelation in question show that it conformed strictly to the law of witnesses. "In the mouth of two or three witnesses shall every word be established" (2 Cor.13:1; Deut. 17:6; 19:15; Matt. 18:16; John 8:12-19). Elder Bruce R. McConkie, in discussing this law at greater length, confines its application to the establishment of a new dispensation or to the conferring of priesthood and keys upon men, "thus leaving their hearers without excuse in the day of judgment should the testimony be rejected."[29] Although Section 76 did not involve the conferring of priesthood keys, it could certainly be argued that it was part of the "establishment of a new dispensation." Moreover, its monumental importance certainly brought its reception within the spirit of the law of witnesses, as do all of the ordinances performed within the temple. By the same token, the truth of the Book of Mormon was confirmed in a spectacularly marvelous manner by the testimony of the three and the eight witnesses.

I now briefly discuss a third episode (out of many more), referred to above, in which more than the Prophet himself beheld the Father and the Son during the pre-temple period in Kirtland. It occurred in the following year, on March 18, 1833, and the occasion was the setting apart of the members of the First Presidency, namely Sidney Rigdon and Frederick G. Williams. On that occasion the Prophet recorded: "Many of the brethren saw a heavenly vision of the Savior, and concourses of angels, and many other things, of which each one has a record of what he saw."[30]

Zebedee Coltrin was one of those attending the above meeting and who "recorded what he saw." Here are the words which he used to describe this experience. After seeing both the Savior and the Father, he said:

> Who [referring to the Father] was surrounded as with a flame of fire which was so brilliant that I could not discover anything else but His person. I saw His hands, His legs, His feet, His eyes, nose, mouth, head, and body in the shape and form of a perfect man.
>
> This appearance was so grand and overwhelming that it seemed I should melt down in his presence. And the sensation was so powerful that it thrilled through my whole system. And I felt it in the marrow of my bones. . . .[31]

The Kirtland Temple

With that, we shall continue with our story of the Kirtland Temple. That brings us to Section 95 of the Doctrine and Covenants, which was given on June 1, 1833. Remember that in Section 88, dated December 27, 1832, the Prophet was told to establish a house of God (temple). Now, five months later, the Saints are reprimanded by the Lord in Section 95. In effect, he is saying: "Where is my temple? You haven't even started." And that was correct, they hadn't started. They had formed a committee, headed by Hyrum Smith, and had done some work raising funds, with modest success, but no rocks had been quarried, no dirt moved, no foundations laid—nothing. So, six months later, the Lord reprimands them:

> Wherefore, ye must needs be chastened and stand rebuked before my face; for ye have sinned against me a very grievous sin, in that ye have not considered the great commandment in all things, that I have given unto you concerning the building of mine house. (D&C 95:2-3)

The record shows that after that the Prophet did not have to be told twice. On June 5, 1833, (five days after receiving Section 95) "George A. Smith hauled the first load of stone for the Temple and Hyrum Smith and Reynolds Cahoon commenced digging the trench for the walls of the Lord's house, and finished the same with their own hands."[32]

Before tracing the progress of the construction, it would first be appropriate to discuss the rest of Section 95. As stated above, the Saints were told to proceed without delay. That in itself was of the utmost importance. It showed that the Lord was following a rigid timetable, which had to become the Saints' timetable! In that same section, the Lord also talks about the endowment. The word "endowment," as it appears there, is not used in quite the same sense as it is used today. Its meaning has evolved since then. At that time, the word was used with the general meaning of an "outpouring of spiritual power from on high" given to strengthen those who covenanted to serve the Lord in righteousness. The ordinance of the endowment, as we now use the term, did not come until later. None of the temple ordinances as we know them today were known at that time, except for the ordinances of washing and anointing which came into being about the time of the Kirtland Temple's completion. They were the beginnings of that full panoply of ordinances which came with the Nauvoo Temple.

Now Section 95 also gives some information about the temple itself, such as its dimensions and the like. The building was to have three floors, the bottom being for general meetings—sacrament meetings and the like, and the second floor was for the School of the Apostles. No mention is made, there, of the use for which the third floor was intended. The facts are that it was divided up into a number of smaller rooms which were used for priesthood quorum activities, and for performing special ordinances, receiving special revelations, and for carrying on administrative functions.

Having received authorization, the Saints proceeded to build the temple. They chose the most elevated site possible, although the general evenness of the terrain did not allow for any considerable degree of elevation. This followed accepted temple procedure because, as pointed out in chapter two, temples have always been built on the highest site available. It is interesting to note that from the top of the Kirtland temple on a clear day one can see Lake Erie, about six miles away.

In the early stages, some of the brethren suggested to the Prophet that the temple be built out of logs. The Prophet's response was, in effect: "No, absolutely not. The house of God is entitled to something much better than that." So it was built out of a good-quality gray stone. They found a rock quarry north of the city which could supply them with what they needed. Even the Prophet himself, to set a good example, descended into the quarry, appropriately dressed, and did his bit to hack out chunks of stone appropriate for trimming and installation, although he had never before had experience in this type of labor.

Most Latter-day Saints have seen pictures of the Kirtland Temple which show it to be surfaced with brick. Actually, it has undergone several transformations, including a resurfacing of the exterior facade. The original exterior, however, was definitely made of grey stone, covered with plaster. Most of us have also heard the story of the sisters who ground up their chinaware and added it to the plaster mix to make the exterior glisten. Brother Karl R. Anderson did some research on the matter. His conclusion: "There is no evidence to either affirm or disaffirm that story. If you wish to go on believing it, there is no one who will ever prove you to be wrong."

What we do know, however, is that the building was constructed at great sacrifice, and that the sisters, in doing what they were best qualified to do (raising money and knitting clothes for the brethren) made as significant a contribution as did the brethren.

In considering the difficulties which the Saints encountered as they pressed forward with the construction, let us pause for a moment to visualize the situation as it was. Many of the Saints were living a hand-to-mouth existence, having recently arrived from New York, bringing with them few of their material possessions. Even the others had accumulated very little wealth, and obtaining the necessary bank-credit was next to impossible. Moreover, sheer economic survival had to become everyone's top priority.

The temple was projected to become a large and imposing building. The required manual skills and equipment for a construction on this scale were almost totally lacking. Technology was primitive, to say the least. In 1833 they had no power-driven machines for lifting, no trucks for hauling, and no modern tools or implements for making construction easier and faster. Even more important than that, there were very few with any experience in large-scale construction, and there was no one at all to serve as an experienced construction foreman. Realizing the difficulty, someone informed the Prophet that he knew of a Canadian named Artemis Millet who had functioned as a construction foreman. However, he was not a member of the Church. The Prophet thereupon called his informant on a mission to go to Canada and to convert Mr. Millet. "And by the way," added the Prophet, "tell him to bring with him a thousand dollars." God did move in a mysterious way, his wonders to perform, for both of those objectives were realized.

The task was further complicated by the hostility which the non-Latter-day Saint neighbors evinced toward the project. From the very start they were opposed to it and immediately launched a campaign of serious harassment. This would make a sidebar story all in itself. Many of these non-members had sworn on oath that they would stop at nothing to prevent the Mormons from completing their temple. Heber C. Kimball related that frequently the workers had to carry loaded muskets and other weapons with them as a protection against the predations of their enemies.

Then, about half-way through the construction period, there occurred the Zion's Camp episode, whose sad but inspiring story fills a number of pages in the annals of church history. But the expedition drained off about 200 of the region's most able-bodied men, who marched off to Missouri to try to rescue the beleaguered Saints there. Their absence greatly diminished the availability of manpower in Kirtland for a considerable period.

These, then, are just some of the difficulties the Saints encountered. And yet, in spite of them, the temple was finally completed in January of 1836. Starting from the moment of the turning of the first spade of earth, and ending at the moment of placing the final touches on the finished building, the temple construction consumed about 33 months. This has to be considered a miracle; of that there can be no question on the part of any fair-minded person. The Lord, without any doubt, gave to his willing servants the help they needed to surmount the most intractable of obstacles, and to meet the decreed deadline (D&C 95:11). In less than three months after completion, the temple was destined to become the site for one of the most historic and watershed events in the history of the Church, namely the transmittal of the keys for performing the temple ordinances of exaltation for the dead.

This was the ecstasy which constitutes the theme of this chapter. It was as though the Lord had given special consideration to the Saints who had sacrificed so much and who had put forth such a monumental effort to do what had been asked of them. Furthermore, the completion of the construction of the temple in record time was followed by a series of circumstances in connection with its dedication that were so transcendently glorious that an account of them could only do them justice by comparing them favorably to the Pentecostal outpouring referred to in the second chapter of the Book of Acts, or to the spiritual outpouring at the dedication of the temple of Solomon, referred to in 1 Kings, Chapter 8. It was a repeat of those historic events, but in a modern setting.

Miracles in the Kirtland Temple

Church historians record a number of occasions when both the Father and the Son appeared, *within the temple itself,* during this period of miraculous outpourings. I shall discuss only two. The first occurred on January 21, 1836. The Saints had already moved in to occupy the building, though it would not be dedicated for another two months. There may have been a little more trimming yet to be done, and the date for the dedication had not yet been fixed. Being desperately in need of more room, the Saints took advantage of the available space and started to put the building to good use.

On this particular day we are told that the First Presidency and the Twelve first met in the afternoon. The meeting actually was not held in the temple itself, to begin with, but in an adjacent building, which was used for housing a printing press and for other purposes. There they washed themselves with pure water. Following that, they moved over into the temple. When evening came, they proceeded to perform the second step in the ordinance which had started with the washing, namely their anointing with consecrated oil. They had been joined in the meantime by Patriarch Joseph Smith Sr., the Prophet's father, and by other

Church leaders. The scene was thus set for a marvelous manifestation of celestial light and glory. It was then that the Prophet received the revelation, a portion of which is now identified as the Doctrine and Covenants, Section 137, and a portion of which section reads as follows:

> The heavens were opened upon us, and I beheld the celestial kingdom of God, and the glory thereof, whether in the body or out I cannot tell. I saw the transcendent beauty of the gate through which the heirs of that kingdom will enter, which was like unto circling flames of fire; also the blazing throne of God, whereon was seated the Father and the Son. I saw the beautiful streets of that kingdom, which had the appearance of being paved with gold. I saw . . . my father and my mother; my brother Alvin, that has long since slept; and marveled how it was that he had obtained an inheritance in that kingdom, seeing that he had departed this life before the Lord had set his hand to gather Israel the second time, and had not been baptized for the remission of sins. Thus came the voice of the Lord unto me, saying "All who have died without a knowledge of this gospel, who would have received it if they had been permitted to tarry, shall be heirs of the celestial kingdom of God. . . ." (vv. 1-7)

Now the curious thing is that the Prophet was seeing what seemed to him to be the Celestial Kingdom, and in it he saw not only his mother and father, but his brother Alvin. It must be recalled, however, that his father was sitting right there by him, and his mother was not far away, yet he saw both of them and his brother Alvin in his vision, all at the same time. The latter had been perhaps the favorite among the Smiths' numerous progeny. He was the oldest, but had died in 1823, and therefore had only an inkling of the great work that yet lay before his younger brother Joseph.

But the Prophet was very concerned lest his brother Alvin, whom he loved dearly, and who apparently had been a most remarkable young man, not having been baptized, might be forever barred from the Celestial Kingdom. So this vision was given him, in effect, to reassure him that Alvin was not barred.

The question arises, was Alvin in the Celestial Kingdom *at that moment of time* even though he had not yet been baptized, and even though no temple ordinances of exaltation had been performed in his behalf? The language of the revelation does not say that Alvin was *then* in the Celestial Kingdom, but that he would qualify to become an *heir* to that Kingdom if he "would have received it" [this gospel] had he heard it. It would seem quite obvious that the Prophet's vision was not one of the Celestial Kingdom as it was constituted *at that moment of time* because the vision included his father who, at that moment was sitting right there by his side. The word "heir" is the key word to our understanding of the revelation. Attorneys understand that an heir to an inheritance does not yet have a vested right to it, but an inchoate right, meaning that it is not completely vested, but that there yet awaits the occurrence of some future events before the vesting becomes absolute. The testator must first die, without having altered the will in the meantime, and the estate must be probated.

In the case of Alvin, what would yet have to take place before his inheritance would vest was the performance of the temple ordinances of exaltation on his behalf by proxy. Nothing in this revelation suggested that the Lord was carving out an exception to the general rule that temple ordinances are a prerequisite for achieving exaltation in the highest kingdom of glory (except for the special rule for infants).

How appropriate, then, that this revelation was given in the very temple, and almost at the very moment, when Elijah conveyed the keys authorizing the commencement of the great work for the exaltation of the dead.

The Kirtland Temple Dedication

The dedication of the temple involves my second example of a celestial experience falling within the time framework we are considering. (The events dealt with in Section 110 of the Doctrine and Covenants are a special case, and will be treated separately in chapter 7.) This was an extraordinary event, long looked forward to by the faithful Saints. It took place on Sunday, March 27, 1836. The date is significant. There were 900 people in attendance. Those who have visited the temple in recent years can see for themselves that there is no way in which 900 people could have fit into the available seats in the room where the dedicatory services were held. The explanation must be that children were allowed to sit on laps if they could behave themselves. It is said that every lap was occupied by a child. Even then, many hopefuls were disappointed because of the insufficiency of the space, so a second session was held for them at a later date.

The dedication service proceeded somewhat as follows. President Sidney Rigdon, a first counselor in the First Presidency, gave the master sermon. It lasted two and a half hours and was built on the theme that "Foxes have holes and birds of the air have nests, but the Son of Man hath not where to lay his head." He pointed out that in ancient times there had been temples where God could come down to make his presence felt, but they had become apostate, or "desolate."A desolate temple is one that no longer has authority to perform its sacred functions. Now a new temple was completed which would enable Jehovah to once again speak to his people and authorize the performance of sacred ordinances.

The congregation then sang "Now Let us Rejoice," whose words had recently been written by W.W. Phelps. Then came the sustaining of officers. Following that, the Prophet Joseph Smith spoke briefly. Then came the dedicatory prayer, and that, of course, was the climax of the entire dedicatory service. In it, the Prophet, after expressing gratitude for God's blessings and with hands raised to heaven and tears flowing freely, prayed that the Lord would accept the temple which had been built after much tribulation, that the Son of Man might have a place to manifest himself to his people. Thus the Kirtland temple, like holy sanctuaries of old, became a place of revelation from God to man.

Following that, the choir sang "The Spirit of God Like a Fire Is Burning," which has become traditional in every temple dedication ever since. That was the musical high point of the service, and the hearts of those in attendance were bursting with joy, their tears flowing in rivulets as they experienced the sublime emotional climax following the difficult ordeals which had preceded it.

Following that, the sacrament was administered and distributed. Afterwards, the Prophet testified that he had seen heavenly personages during the service. The meeting concluded with the congregation standing and rendering the hosanna shout—*Hosanna, Hosanna, Hosanna to God and the Lamb, amen, amen, and amen,* repeated three times. That must have been an unforgettable moment. After seven hours the meeting finally adjourned, and the brethren and sisters went home, with their children who had been sitting so patiently on their laps. One can only wonder how their physical selves had been able to endure such physical punishment, but apparently that's the way they did things in 1833. As an interesting footnote, the Prophet had sent out instructions to those of the prospective congregation, prior to the dedication, saying, in effect, "I want you to come prepared." In what way were they to come prepared? First, they were to be "solemn." That is to say, they were to put aside light-mindedness. Solemn did not mean long-faced. In this context, it just meant that they were to be thinking about serious things because this was to be a serious occasion.

Second, they were to come purified and sanctified, that they might be worthy to bear the vessels of the Lord. The purification was to be physical as well as spiritual. We find frequent references in contemporary literature to the need for physical cleanliness. Today, we take cleanliness almost for granted. It must be remembered that in the 1830's, the physical amenities of life were crude by our standards, and the facilities for washing and bathing were primitive, at best. The daily shower, which is today's necessity, in those days was unknown.

And third, they were to have studied the commandments and the pertinent revelations on the subject, having pondered and prayed about them. So, having done those three things, the Prophet told them, they would be prepared to come and participate in this historic dedicatory service.

The Prophet's dedicatory prayer, as an expression of fervent supplication, was in a class by itself, as well it should be, since it had been revealed to the Prophet, word for word, by the Lord himself. It was masterful in its sonorities and recalled the majestic cadences of the Old Testament prophets at their best. It has become the model for subsequent temple dedicatory prayers.

The prayer, reproduced in Section 109 of the Doctrine and Covenants, should be read by every temple-goer.

Those who have attended a modern temple dedication recall that they are requested to come equipped with a clean white handkerchief. At the appropriate moment they are directed to joyfully wave it in the air while repeating the hosanna shout. This practice had its origin with the Kirtland Temple dedication, and has been continued ever since. It is symbolic not only of Old Testament practices, but recalls the royal reception and greeting accorded the Savior by his followers at his entry into Jerusalem on Palm Sunday. The Hebrew word "hosanna"embraces both the meaning of "Save me for I need your help"and "Welcome (to the King)." How appropriate!

During the few weeks following the dedication, Kirtland seemed to be a foretaste of paradise. As Dr. Truman Madsen pointed out, the members thought they had reached the very threshold of the Millennium. Stories abound concerning some members' going about visiting other members with the message: "I have a blessing for you," to which the ones visited would respond with "And I have a blessing for you, too." The Mormon community had found peace, at last, and heaven seemed not very far away.

More specifically, during the week following the dedication, and within the sacred temple walls, a series of miracles, angelic apparitions, and theophanies occurred which were without parallel in all of recorded sacred history. Every day seemed to bring with it some unprecedented marvel, which left the Saints in joyous stupefaction.

Eliza R. Snow, in her *Biography of Lorenzo Snow,* p. 11, states that President Snow enumerated some of the blessings received in the temple during this Pentecostal period. They included the gift of prophecy and of tongues, the gift of the interpretation of tongues, visions, and marvelous dreams, the singing of heavenly choirs, and wonderful manifestations of the healing power through the administration of the Elders. The sick were healed, the deaf were made to hear, the blind to see, and the lame to walk.

According to President Snow, the Savior appeared alone in five different meetings held in the temple during this brief period. Visions, including a vision of the Father and the Son together, were beheld at eight meetings, and the congregations saw heavenly beings, or angels, in nine meetings.

The list could go on. We are reminded of that comparable celebratory event occurring 3,000 years ago, involving the dedication of the Temple of Solomon, once the glory of Israel, but now buried in the dust forever. "And it came to pass, when the priests were come out of the holy place, that the cloud [i.e., pillar of brilliant light] filled the house of the Lord, so that the priests could not stand to minister because of the cloud [pillar of light]: for the glory of the Lord had filled the house of the Lord" (1 Kings 8:10-11).

Whether we are talking of Solomon's temple or of the modern temple in Kirtland, the unprecedented outpouring of these signs and wonders in both cases was evidence that each one had been accepted by the Great Jehovah and was endowed with authority to perform ordinances in his name.

To this point, only scant reference has been made to the most important single event to occur in the Kirtland Temple, described Section 110 of the Doctrine and Covenants. It constituted the temple's climactic event, surpassing in importance all the others considered together, which occurred within the walls of this sacred building. Its significance is so monumental that a fuller discussion of it must be reserved for chapter 7. It was the event in which the Savior Jesus Christ appeared, followed by Moses, Elias, and the Prophet Elijah, who conveyed the keys authorizing this generation to initiate the great work for the dead. Those keys were bestowed upon the Prophet Joseph Smith and were subsequently transmitted, in proper sequence, to Joseph Smith's successors in office, and are held today by the serving President, Prophet, Seer, and Revelator, whomever he may be at the time. This watershed event took place on April 3, 1836, exactly one week following the date of the temple's dedication.

The Ecstasy Turns to Agony

That was the ecstasy. Then came the agony, and it came fast. The Prophet was not taken unawares, however, for he had warned the Saints of what lay ahead. With his prophetic vision, he foresaw the dark clouds and the severe trials and period of testing which yet awaited them. He knew there would be apostasies, and there were.

Elder Boyd K. Packer states: "And here [in Kirtland] apostasy took shape and spread with such power as to eventually compel the Prophet and other leaders to flee to Missouri."[33]

The results of the falling away in 1837-38 by those who could not stand the stress were disastrous. During that period all three of the special witnesses to the Book of Mormon, two of the eight witnesses, and several of the members of the quorum of the twelve became disaffected, or were excommunicated, or both. Other apostasies followed later. Many other members also became disaffected. Bad feelings abounded, and lawsuits were filed. Newton's law of physics, "For every action there is an equal and opposite reaction," was demonstrating its painful application to the laws of human behavior.

It must be emphasized that many of those who fell away came back into the Church and into full fellowship, figuratively crawling on hands and knees, filled with remorse for their transgression. The stories of Oliver Cowdery's and Martin Harris's return to the flock are particularly poignant. Significantly, in spite of the bitterness and discord which Satan had engendered among some of the special witnesses to the Book of Mormon, not one of them ever denied his testimony. Even David Whitmer, who never rejoined the body of the Church, fiercely reaffirmed, time after time, the truth of his original testimony that an angel had appeared and shown him the plates, and that a voice from heaven had confirmed that they had been correctly translated by the gift and power of God. One suspects that the Lord must have told these three men that if they should ever become faithless to the sacred knowledge that had been entrusted to them, they would never be forgiven, either here or hereafter. At least, that's the way they reacted.

The causes for this disaffection were multiple, one of them being petty little differences over turf. Some members, for example, apparently felt that since they had worked on the temple's construction, they had certain proprietary rights to its occupancy, which conflicted with the claims of others who had also worked on its construction. As a result, they carried pistols into the temple itself as a matter of personal protection.

One of the more serious causes of the Kirtland catastrophe, however, was the national bank panic of 1837, which caused the bankruptcy of hundreds of banks nationwide including the one in Kirtland. The latter's failure took with it the investments of a number of church members, causing much hardship, The Prophet Joseph Smith, along with others, had promoted this bank and had a financial interest therein. He also had some responsibilities in the bank's management, which he had performed honorably. It was easy, however, for those who had lost their savings to lash out irresponsibly, and the one bearing the Prophet's mantle inevitably bore the brunt, even though undeservedly.

One might wonder why the Lord did not come to the rescue of his holy temple before it was too late. Exploring the answer to that question would take us far beyond the outer limits of this discussion on the temple. One approach stressed the assurance we have been given by the Savior that our supplications to him, when made in faith, will be granted (Matt. 7:7). The opposite approach emphasized the fact that God will not interfere with the exercise of our own agency, nor will he prevent us from making our own mistakes, for trial and error is the most effective of all learning devices. Each individual, with God's help, will have to reconcile the apparent contradiction between these two approaches.

In passing, it might be commented that the root of the Saints' difficulty may have been the simple fact that they had become greedy. Many of their investments went sour as a result of the national depression of 1837. A financier, today, would probably describe their plight as one of "over-extended and irrational investing, which finally burst their bubble of unrealistic expectations." A spiritually oriented explanation might be that the unprecedented outpouring of heavenly blessings and miracles enjoyed all throughout the previous year should have been followed by a regimen of humiliation and expressions of gratitude for blessings received. Apparently this was not what happened. These lessons came later, but only after some of the Saints left their footprints stained with blood in the snow. This was literally true in the case of certain members of the unfortunate Willey and Martin handcart companies in 1856, whose faith, for the most part, became strengthened rather than weakened from their ordeal.

Let us not exaggerate the extent of the Saints' defection. The most impressive aspect of the entire Kirtland episode was not that some members apostatized, but that so many did not. In the face of massive disappointments and discouragement, most still remained stalwart in their faith. They followed the Prophet in his exodus from Kirtland, firm in the absolute conviction that the Lord was leading him and them by the hand, to the fulfillment of their divinely-appointed destiny.

The historical threads become very tangled at this juncture because of events occurring simultaneously in Missouri and in Kirtland and the interaction between these two Latter-day Saint communities. In a moment, this aspect of the story will be pursued.

We could try, perhaps fruitlessly, to reach a consensus on why the Kirtland establishment unraveled at the end, leading to its evacuation and the abandonment of its crown jewel, the temple. So many wonderful things had been promised for it which were never realized (D&C 110:7-10). Each historian will have his own explanation. One of them might be that the Prophet, in choosing his leaders at the very outset, had an extremely narrow spectrum of available choices. During all of the New York and part of the Kirtland periods, the entire church membership did not exceed that of one of today's stakes. Out of that pitifully small population base he was required to find the cadre upon whose shoulders he could lay the complex organizational structure of the entire Church. Most of the leaders so chosen were young men. A large number of them were under thirty, and most of them were less than forty. Many were farmers or tradesmen by occupation, with only a rudimentary formal education and little or no professional training.

Reading between the lines, we deduce that certain understandable jealousies must have reared their heads. Those who had become leaders at the very threshold when there was only a handful of candidates to pick from saw themselves being replaced by more competent or stronger members after the Church's numbers had increased. This was the result of the painful but inevitable sifting process experienced by every growing organization, in which the less effective are replaced by the more effective.

Considering Satan's determined effort to destroy the infant Church at whatever cost, and the natural trials and obstacles which the Church was required to face, the miracle is that so many leaders and members did stand firm as a rock through thick and thin and successfully met every test to which they were put.

I am firmly convinced, moreover, that not only did the Lord raise up a special generation to create our constitutional form of government (D&C 101:80), but that he also raised up an equally special generation to nurture the restored Church during its birth and infancy. The outstanding success which these men and women achieved bespeaks their far-above-average intelligence and abilities plus the inspiration which they enjoyed throughout their perilous journeys. But they were human, nevertheless, and internecine tensions were inevitable.

We must also remember that the Lord is still using Kirtland to send out a message to those of us who follow. That message is that the faith that is built up on wonders and miracles alone, even the Kirtland-type spectaculars, is never robust enough to survive by itself. Moreover, even spectacular miracles themselves do not convert those whose minds are set against it. Experience shows us that we believe what we want to believe. It is interesting to note that even though some of the miracles associated with the dedication of the Kirtland temple, such as the appearance of angels and heavenly lights, were clearly seen and noted from the outside by non-members, yet we have no record of any of these non-members lining up the following morning to apply for baptism. They may have been impressed, but they were not converted.

That is exactly what happened in ancient times as well. In John 12:37 we read: "But though he [the Savior] had done so many miracles before them, yet they believed not on him."

Recall what the situation was which gives us the context for that verse. The Savior, on the Sunday preceding his crucifixion, entered Jerusalem on a donkey and the crowds thronged adoringly around him, giving him the welcome reserved for kings. They had heard of the miracles he had performed, particularly of the raising of Lazarus after four days in the tomb. This spectacular miracle was common talk in Jerusalem, and the people were impressed. And yet when the crunch came, five days later, how many were there among Jesus' adorers who came to his defense when Pilate put the latter's fate into their hands? The answer is "Not one."

The message is clear. A faith built *exclusively* on miracles does not have a sufficiently solid foundation to survive the trials and temptations that Satan will inflict on those who have received the miracles. In answer to the oft-asked question: "Why doesn't the Lord make it easier for us to develop our faith by giving us more miracles?" the definitive response is found in the Book of Mormon:

> . . . I would show unto the world that faith is things which are hoped for and not seen; wherefore, dispute not because ye see not, for ye receive no witness *until after the trial of your faith.* (Ether 12:6, emphasis added)

The British Mission

Before leaving the Kirtland period, let me add an additional inspirational footnote which relates to it. In 1837, probably the most disappointing year in the Church's history, the Prophet took the riskiest step that he could possibly have taken. He announced to the world, in effect: "The Lord wants me to organize the British Mission. To that end, he wants me to send some of my very best men to England: Heber C. Kimball, Orson Hyde, Willard Richards, and Joseph Fielding." They were followed, two years later, by other giants, and before the end of 1840 almost every member of the Quorum of the Twelve had done missionary service in Great Britain.

This was madness! Human logic would have said: "Hey! This is the worst possible period. Your timing is terrible. Keep your troops at home. You need all the loyal men and women you can afford, right here. This is your low point. Hunker down. Consolidate your strength. Circle the wagons, and wait for the onslaught of the enemy." But the Lord knew something that human beings did not know: that Great Britain was a huge fertile field, ripe for the harvest. So, faced with protestations to the contrary, the Prophet reaffirmed: "No, you are wrong. The Lord has told me to organize the British Mission." This was a miraculous insight, far exceeding in importance many of the more spectacular ones, as is borne out by the following statistic:

LDS Church Membership in 1851

Location	***Membership***
Utah	12,000
United Kingdom & Ireland	33,000

Source: *Encyclopedia of Mormonism,* vol. 1, p. 227

The British Saints provided the infusion of new membership which the Church needed to survive the rough days that lay ahead. Once again the Lord's wisdom overruled man's wisdom, and the Prophet Joseph Smith showed the spiritual sensitivity to recognize it and to act accordingly. Perhaps he recalled what the Lord had told him seven years previously: "I will not suffer that they shall destroy my work; yea, I will show unto them that *my wisdom is greater than the cunning of the devil*" (D&C 10:43, emphasis added).

The Missouri Episode

Let us now turn our attention, for a moment, to Missouri. We tend to overlook the fact that during this Kirtland period there were really two major centers of Church activity—one in Kirtland and the other in Missouri. We cannot exactly call the latter a Church headquarters, for that honor belonged to Kirtland, but we must recognize that Missouri was invested with an overall importance in the larger picture that exceeded even that of Kirtland.

In Missouri the Saints ultimately found the fulfillment of both ancient and modern prophecies regarding the establishment of a holy city, a city of Enoch and a gathering place for the righteous from all over the world. There the Saints found peace and a refuge from the storm, while all the rest of the world was torn apart by strife and dissension.

In addition, the greatest of latter-day temples was presumably to be constructed, from which would go forth the law according to Isaiah's famous prophecy (Isaiah 2:3). During most of the 1830's, although the majority of the members were physically present in Kirtland, the spiritual focus was on Missouri. To that place a goodly number of Saints had already moved where their own history played out, which turned out to be even more tumultuous than that of Kirtland.

In the revelation contained in the Doctrine and Covenants 28:9, received in 1830, the Lord made known to the Prophet that Zion was to be established and would be located "on the borders, by the Lamanites." This was consistent with the Book of Mormon's prediction that Zion would be established "in this land" (3 Nephi 21:1, 4). A more precise location, however, was not indicated at that time.

The following summer the Prophet himself visited this area. The missionary foursome previously referred to (that included Parley P. Pratt) was already there and greeted him when he arrived. There, on July 30, 1831, as recorded in Doctrine and Covenants 57:1-2, the Lord at long last more clearly unveiled the whole concept of the city of Zion and indicated with precision where it, and the temple itself, were to be located. The city was to be at Independence, Jackson County, Missouri, and the temple site was a half mile west of the Independence courthouse.

Three days later, on August 3, 1831, the Prophet dedicated the ground and laid the foundation for the erection of the Independence, Missouri temple. This was a year and a half before any specific mention was made of a temple in Kirtland, so for the time being, all of the Saints' attention was focused on the forthcoming one in Independence. The dedication of the site and the groundbreaking, which followed a rigidly prescribed ritual, got things off to a good start. As a result, there followed a great influx of members into Missouri. This was both good and bad: good, because the objective of the Church was, and still remains, to bring the gospel of salvation to as many people as possible; bad, because the great influx aroused the suspicions and animosities of the neighbors in that area.

Central and western Missouri then formed part of the great American frontier. Frontiers are notorious for attracting a distinctive type of people. Trying to avoid being judgmental, I believe it can be safely said that the moral standards of many of those who fled to the frontier to escape the restrictions and penalties imposed by a more settled society in the east were such that they were not always proponents of tolerance and peace.

Nor all Missourians were of questionable morals, for there were many among them who were good solid citizens. Actually, Missouri's population was a mixture, but there were enough of the untamed element to make certain that the incoming Mormons were perpetually forced to defend themselves.

To some degree that explains the underlying reason for the hostility demonstrated by the native Missourians, which almost immediately flared up. The more immediate cause of this hostility were the religious and cultural disparities (particularly on the issue of slavery) between the older settlers and the newcomers. The result was that the saints in Jackson County were never able to carry through on the construction of their temple. After dedicating the ground and laying the cornerstone, they could go no further. A short time later they were physically driven out of Jackson County, after which they fled, successively, to Ray County, Clay County, and finally to Caldwell County.

For a while, things were reasonably peaceful. In fact (and this is something that most Latter-day Saints have forgotten), they were told by the Lord to build another temple, this time in Far West, Caldwell County, Missouri. So on July 4, 1838, the ground was dedicated for its erection, during which ceremony the prescribed formalities were scrupulously followed. But its eventual fate was the same as it had been in Jackson County, that is, the temple never happened. Why? Because the saints' expulsion from Missouri following the infamous extermination order of Governor Lilburn Boggs made it impossible for construction even to begin.

Why did the Lord ask the Saints to undertake a task that was obviously impossible for them to perform? The answer to that question, however, was clearly given and is found in D&C 124:49. The Lord there tells the Saints that when he gives them a task to do, and when they labor with all their might to perform that task but are prevented by enemies who make its completion impossible, then the Lord relieves them from the responsibility for their failure. This is a pivotal point in properly interpreting the events which were to follow. The scene now shifts eastward to the Saints' brand new home in Illinois.

5
Nauvoo

A City Is Born

In 1839 the Missouri Saints, their ranks swollen by a massive influx of Kirtland exiles, came straggling into their new refuge in Illinois like a battered army. When, in 1831, they had tried to create a Zion community in Jackson County, what they expected was a Shangri-la of pure love and domestic tranquility, a veritable city of Enoch. What they actually got was a string of nasty conflicts with their hostile neighbors, eventuating in open warfare. Blood was spilled, lives were lost. Now they were moving again, most of them for the fourth time, and some for the fifth or sixth.

The plight of these wayfarers of misfortune was shared by the Prophet himself, who had just been released from a foul prison after having been incarcerated there for over five months on falsified charges. His plight was expressed three years later by O. H. Browning, the attorney who defended him in an Illinois court against an unlawful extradition order requiring him to return again to Missouri to answer further trumped-up charges:

> Great God! Have I not seen it? Yes, my eyes have beheld the blood-stained tracks of innocent women and children, in the dreary winter, who had traveled hundreds of miles barefoot, through frost and snow, to seek a refuge from their savage pursuers. 'Twas a scene of horror sufficient to enlist sympathy from an adamantine heart. And shall this unfortunate man, whom their fury has been proper to select for sacrifice, be driven into such a savage land and none dare to enlist in the cause of Justice? If there were no other voice under heaven ever to be heard in this cause, gladly would I stand alone, and proudly spend my latest breath in defense of an oppressed American citizen.

Physically exhausted, dispirited, and stripped of almost all their possessions, including tools, agricultural implements, and livestock, this battered army found itself facing a bleak and uncertain future in a new state, but one beguiling enough to induce them to make still another try. The Mormon odyssey was full of miracles, and their tenacity at this juncture was certainly one of them, growing out of an almost unparalleled faith in God and in his prophet Joseph Smith. In spite of their physical disability and state of demoralization, they miraculously rallied, and, within the following six years, cleared a swamp and replaced it with a community of 20,000 persons. They called it Nauvoo. This community was among the largest and fastest-growing on the western frontier in the early 1840's. But the miracle of its creation was surpassed by a still greater one.

The Vision of a New Temple

Early in 1840, having just recently arrived in Nauvoo, the Prophet Joseph Smith gave a discourse on the principle of temple building. He said: "Now, brethren, I obligate myself to build as great a temple as ever Solomon did, if the Church will back me up. . . . And if it should be the will of God that I might live to behold that temple completed and finished from the foundation to the top stone, I will say: 'O Lord, it is enough. Let thy servant depart in peace.' . . ."[34]

At General Conference, October 3-5, 1840, the Prophet preached on the necessity of building a house of the Lord in Nauvoo.[35]

From that date until his death in 1844, building a new temple became almost an obsession with him. What makes the whole episode so miraculous is that the Church *did* back him up. At the church conference of October 6, 1840, the members voted to commence work on the temple. Their subsequent deeds matched their words, for plans were immediately drawn up. By March 1, 1841, construction was under way and the dirt had begun to fly. This continued until the temple was finally dedicated five-and-a-half years later.

To measure the magnitude of this miracle one must step back for a moment to survey the situation as it was then. Picture the bleak circumstances in which the Saints found themselves in early 1840. They were still licking their Missouri-inflicted wounds. Several of their leaders had been killed or had died from the ill effects of the savaging they had received, including David Patten, Edward Partridge, and their beloved Patriarch Joseph Smith Sr. To make matters worse, several pivotal leaders had forsaken the Church, including all three of the special witnesses to the Book of Mormon as well as several of the eight witnesses and apostles. This had been terribly demoralizing. Moreover, the Saints found themselves still without financial savings or credit, their homes unbuilt, tool sheds unstocked, livestock unreplenished, and fields uncleared or uncultivated.

Now consider the fact that practical, common sense was the law of survival on the American frontier in 1840. Had the Saints been driven exclusively by that type of frontier common sense, their reaction to the prophet's request that they build a temple the size of Solomon's may have been something like this:

> In the last eight years we have suffered three bitter disappointments as far as temples are concerned. The first was in Kirtland, where the temple we built at great effort and sacrifice was miserably abandoned. Two more were in Missouri, where we scarcely got started before we were driven away at gunpoint by our enemies. Now, the Prophet is asking us to get mixed up in a fourth, which seems to us to be just another wild adventure. As for starting this immediate construction, the timing couldn't be worse. Please, Brother Joseph, give us two or three years more time: time for our wounds to heal, time to build our homes and barns, and schools, and stores, time to plant our crops, and to construct an infrastructure of roads and fences and ditches. In a word, give us time to get back to normal living. Then we will think about undertaking another ambitious venture.

But there's the miracle, for *that isn't the way they reacted at all.* Their faith overruled their common sense. What would ordinarily have been considered the only reasonable attitude for them to take yielded to the will of God, which even the secular historians must acknowledge to have been a most extraordinary, if not miraculous, turn of events which none of them could have predicted. Apparently the Saints had faith that the Lord would help them do the impossible.

From an LDS retrospective point of view, we now realize how clearly the Lord knew certain things which the Saints did not know at the time, but had to accept on faith. Going back nine years, just as the construction of the Kirtland temple had to be undertaken on faith and finished within the allotted three-and-a-half-year window of time so that Elijah could transfer certain keys to Joseph Smith before the temple had to be abandoned, so the construction of the much larger Nauvoo temple had to be undertaken within a narrow six-year window of time so that the Saints could receive their soon-to-be-revealed sacred temple ordinances before *their* temple would have to be abandoned. Their window of time was relatively small, and they had to move quickly before it was too late. The point is that the Lord was setting a course of action directed by circumstances about which the Saints had no knowledge at that time. God well knew that Nauvoo was destined to spring up out of nothing, to then reach full bloom, and finally to wither away, all within the space of six years. He also knew that the Saints, after being forced to abandon the city and the temple which they had so lovingly built, would then be cut off from any other temple for years to come.

But he could not allow them to be swallowed up in the wilderness without first taking with them at least some familiarity with temple ordinances, and without having received the strength which the temple ordinances would give them.

After these ordinances were resumed, thirty-two years after the exodus, it would be necessary for temple officiators, and particularly Brigham Young, who held all the necessary keys, to act as the connecting link between the Nauvoo temple and the temples of the future. God, being omniscient, knew all this but the Saints did not. But what they *did* know was that God, speaking through his Prophet, would guide them aright. They did what they knew had to be done, even though they may not have fully known the reason.

But the Saints had their faults, too, and we distort our historical perspective by assuming they did not. It is this fact that makes the experience all the more dramatic and gives it more meaning for us. The fact that their faith was strong did not mean that they were transformed, *ipso facto,* into angels. We are dealing here with mortal human beings. As they plodded on with their construction work, their human weaknesses caught up with them, just as ours do with us. They faced poor working conditions, inferior tools, low pay, unequal distribution of provisions, and mistaken appropriation of funds. It is true that every able-bodied male member in and around Nauvoo was asked to contribute one day's labor out of every ten, without pay, to the construction of the temple. Most of them did. The temple could never have been built without this kind of help, nor without the generosity shown by so many men and women in so many other ways. Of necessity a number of professional workers were needed to minimize the mistakes inevitably committed by novices. The Saints were certainly not spared the usual blunders and painful decisions involved in a construction project of this magnitude.

The miracle of the story is that these men and women, being ordinary human beings with the same strengths and weaknesses as everyone else, were nevertheless able to accomplish what seems to us impossible. The saga of the construction of the Nauvoo Temple owes its renown to the fact that it deals with ordinary people, making ordinary mistakes, but having the faith to triumph over extraordinary obstacles. These were not untarnished angels doing everything right. If there was a difference between them and other men and women, it was simply that they really did believe that God would intervene in their behalf to enable them to do what they had to do. They really *did* take the Lord at his word. This same sublime faith was expressed by Nephi who, while crossing the scorching Arabian desert, faced with a seemingly impossible task, said: "And thus we see that the commandments of God must be fulfilled. And if it so be that the children of men keep the commandments of God he doth nourish them, and strengthen them, and provide means whereby they can accomplish the thing which he has commanded them; wherefore, he did provide means for us while we did sojourn in the wilderness" (1 Ne. 17:3).

The Nauvoo miracle, though it manifested itself in visible things such as houses and a mammoth-sized temple, was basically a story of the triumph of the invisible over the visible. The driving force behind these physical accomplishments was a faith that God would do what he said he would do. They knew that the promise previously made to the Kirtlanders applied equally to them: ". . . it is my will that you should build a house. If you keep my commandments *you shall have power to build it*" (D&C 95:11).

It should be mentioned that both the Prophet Joseph Smith and Brigham Young had made occasional statements portending the Church's eventual establishment in the West—Oregon having been specifically mentioned as a possibility. But nothing in their official statements or actions indicated that this was a consideration, as far as the location and the construction of the Nauvoo temple was concerned.

As the Nauvoo period began to wind down, however, the black storm clouds of gathering opposition led to the realization that evacuation would soon become unavoidable. But the Saints' awareness of that fact made their reactions even more incomprehensible to the secular mind. Note that in July 1844, immediately following the Prophet's assassination, and without the slightest idea who the next leader would be, if any (Brigham Young not having returned to Nauvoo until the following month), with the world trumpeting the message that the Church and its Prophet were now dead, work on the construction of the temple continued, *without skipping a beat.* What an astounding fact! Though the Saints began to realize that nobody would be left to enjoy the building after it was completed, the only logic in their continuing to build was that that was what the Lord wanted them to do.

Obedience, however, brought with it a rich payoff. Recorded testimonies abound on the part of those who had to endure the forthcoming exodus to the effect that it was only through the strength which the endowment had given them that the unforgiving rigors of their ordeal became endurable. Some 600 of the Mormon exiles, for example, later perished while shuttling back and forth across the state of Iowa. The survivors of that frightful experience needed the extra strength which the temple experience alone made possible to enable them to sing "All is Well" while burying their loved ones on the desolate western plains.

Temple Doctrine

The Nauvoo period of church history is important to us for a number of reasons which go far beyond that of providing exemplary role models of faith and courage. Two of them are appropriate for discussion in this chapter. The first is the unveiling of new doctrines relating to the ordinances of sealing for time and eternity, endowments, and temple ordinances for the living and the dead; and the second is the giving of the authorization needed for the actual performance of those ordinances—in other words, the transference of the keys of authority. A portion of those temple ordinances, however, had already been revealed and performed in the Kirtland Temple, namely the washing and anointing.

Regarding the newly revealed doctrines relating to the work of the temple, there were a number of them which are here grouped together and presented under four headings. They were not entirely new, it is true, for there had been previous intimations of some of them in the Book of Mormon and elsewhere. But they had never been previously authoritatively and publicly taught in this fashion until Nauvoo. They are as follows:

1. Those who have passed beyond the veil without having received the gospel will have an opportunity of receiving it, and, through the exercise of their agency, of accepting or rejecting it. Thus, death does not write the final chapter in the story of man's struggle to reach eventual exaltation. Opportunities will be given after death to rectify life's inequities and denied opportunities. (See particularly D&C 138.)

2. According to God's plan, wives will eventually be sealed to husbands, and children to parents, for time and eternity, by one having authority, in a temple consecrated to that purpose. These sealings will be performed either in person, while the parties are living, or by proxy after they are deceased.

3. Sacred temple ordinances of exaltation must be received by everyone (infants are subject to a special exception), either personally, if living, or by proxy if deceased. Receiving and accepting these ordinances is a precondition to attaining a celestial glory.

4. Each living person has the responsibility to do what is possible for him, including engaging in family history research, to ensure that his ancestors receive the benefit of the sealing and other temple ordinances referred to above. Eventually, temple work will be done for all who have lived upon the earth.

The human mind finds it impossible to fully grasp the import of the above doctrines, and a fuller discussion of them will be reserved for a later chapter. At this point, however, it must be emphasized that these doctrines are founded on concepts which, in one mighty stroke, attack and destroy the theological misconceptions of misguided dogmatists since the very beginning.

Of special note is the concept that exaltation is multilateral rather than unilateral. These terms are used in the sense that each individual, instead of standing absolutely alone, on the last day of judgment, vis-a-vis his Savior, stands there *with his family and loved ones,* for whose ultimate exaltation he shares a certain inescapable responsibility.

Note the following inspired words taken from Section 128 of the Doctrine and Covenants:

> . . . the earth will be smitten with a curse *unless there is a welding link of some kind or other between the fathers and the children, . . . For we without them cannot be made perfect; neither can they without us be made perfect.* Neither can they nor we be made perfect without those who have died in the gospel also; for it is necessary in the ushering in of the dispensation of the fulness of times, which dispensation is now beginning to usher in, that a whole and complete and perfect *union, and welding together* of dispensations, and keys, and powers, and glories should take place, and be revealed from the days of Adam even to the present time. . . . (D&C 128:18, emphasis added)

For those who have long been immersed in gospel principles, it is difficult to visualize what a complete and distinct break with the past is represented by the Prophet's above-stated position on these foundational issues. The idea that God's children must view themselves as brothers and sisters, united in the total family of God, who is literally our Father in Heaven, and for whose exaltation we bear a measure of responsibility, is so profound and so glorious that the human mind finds itself incapable of grasping its utter magnitude.

The miraculous experiences associated with the performance of these temple ordinances, in which the dead have made known *both their awareness and their approval* of what was being done for them, are so overwhelmingly convincing that no temple worker who is truly immersed in the work can doubt its efficacy in accomplishing its designated purpose.

The Prophet Joseph Smith, early in his Nauvoo residency, was told by the Lord that certain sacred temple ordinances had to be received (with a special exception for infants) before a person could enter into his celestial glory. These ordinances included baptism, confirmation (receiving the Holy Ghost; see *Fourth Article of Faith*), receiving the priesthood (for men), sealing for time and eternity, and that ordinance which has come to be known as the endowment, including the initiatory ordinances.

At the time the prophet received knowledge of the above temple ordinances, he also became aware that they could only be performed in a holy temple. We have reason to believe, from parenthetical words which he spoke from time to time, that he had a premonition of his forthcoming and premature death. The prophet, faced with this troubling awareness and with the realization that there was no temple on the earth in which these sacred ordinances could be performed, realized further the necessity of having them performed before he died, and of transmitting the authority given to him by Elijah for their performance, to his successors. He was thus almost obsessed with the need for finishing the temple within the small framework of time that yet remained.

Some concessions to reality had to be made to move things along. Let's take baptism for the dead as an example. On August 15, 1840, the Prophet preached a sermon at the funeral of one Seymour Brunson. In the congregation was one Jane Neyman who, the Prophet knew, had had a son, then deceased, about whom she worried because he had never been baptized before his death. The Prophet seized the occasion to preach the doctrine of baptism for the dead, which had already been revealed to him. He explained that it was possible for a living person, acting as proxy, to go down into the waters of baptism and be baptized for and on behalf of, a designated deceased person.

No sooner was this delightful news reported to the Church than their reaction was one of ecstasy. Many members had been worried, as the Prophet himself had been, that those of their loved ones who had died without having had a chance to be baptized would be foreclosed forever from the possibility of receiving exaltation.

The inevitable happened. Hundreds of members immediately invaded the shores of the muddy Mississippi River and proceeded to baptize their previously unbaptized deceased loved ones, helter-skelter, brothers being baptized for sisters, and sisters for brothers, and no record whatsoever being kept. It was pure chaos!

This was obviously not according to God's wishes, and he made this fact known. Accordingly, we read in the Doctrine and Covenants, under date of January 19, 1841, the following:

> For a baptismal font there is not upon the earth that they, my saints, may be baptized for those who are dead—For this ordinance belongeth

> to my house, and cannot be acceptable to me, only in the days of your poverty, wherein ye are not able to build a house unto me. . . . But behold, at the end of this appointment your baptisms for your dead shall not be acceptable unto me. . . . (D&C 124:29-32)

At the time that this revelation was given, work on the temple's construction hadn't even begun. It would be five years before it would be completed, and by then the Saints would be in exile. The solution devised was as follows: work hard to complete a sufficiently large portion of the temple to enable baptisms to be performed, even though the rest of the building might not be ready. The portion completed could be dedicated for use in its individualized role, and baptisms could then be performed. So this is exactly what happened, and on November 8, 1841, the temporary font was dedicated, and on the following November 21, baptisms for the dead were performed.

In Section 128 of the Doctrine and Covenants the Saints were advised as follows:

> The baptismal font was instituted as a similitude of the grave, and was commanded to be in a place underneath where the living are wont to assemble, to show forth the living and the dead, and that all things may have their likeness, and that they may accord one with another—that which is earthly conforming to that which is heavenly. . . . (v. 13)

Starting with the Nauvoo Temple, every baptismal font for the dead has been located in the lowest possible portion of the temple structure.

In Section 127 of the Doctrine and Covenants, the Saints were further instructed that when baptisms for the dead were performed, there should in all cases be present a third party who would act both as a witness and a recorder, and that he would carefully keep an accurate record of the proceedings (v. 6).

In the early days of the Church, the rule was that proxy baptisms were to be be performed only for those deceased relatives and ancestors who, the proxy felt, would have accepted the gospel had he heard it preached to him in the flesh. That rule has been modified in recent years. Today, work for the dead can be done for anybody for whom authentic records can be obtained. This is consistent with the principle that ultimately everybody who has ever lived will have to have his or her work done (special rules being applied to infants). If this more modern approach were not adopted, our temples would be virtually empty, since the number of twigs and branches on any given family tree are limited, whereas, if we dip into the larger world-wide pool of names, our resources are unlimited, and no one ever need be turned away from a temple for reasons of insufficiency of names.

Answers to Church Critics

Critics have made much of the fact that the above newly announced doctrines associated with the Nauvoo Temple and its associated ordinances constituted a radical departure or "change" by the Prophet Joseph Smith from the doctrines taught by him prior to the Nauvoo period. The implication is that since God is the same yesterday, today, and forever, he would not be telling the Prophet one thing during the Kirtland period and another thing during the Nauvoo period. They argue that, with specific regard to the above four newly announced temple doctrines, there is not even a suggestion that they existed in the Book of Mormon, or in the Prophet's pre-Nauvoo sermons (which assertion is not factually correct). Therefore, they conclude, the Prophet was fabricating either his Kirtland position or his Nauvoo position, or perhaps both.

This criticism springs from a total misunderstanding of the way in which the Lord communicates to man. When he has messages for his prophet, does he necessarily give them to him *all at once, in their entirety,* thus cutting off all possibility of further elaboration or explanation or enlargement? Of course not! Prophets are human beings, and, like all other human beings, *must go through a learning process*. The Lord, who is the master teacher, proceeds to instruct by building a pyramid of knowledge, starting from the ground up. On the basis of this same principle, a student being instructed in differential calculus must first have been given a foundation in basic mathematics (D&C 93:12-14; Luke 2:52; Heb. 5:8-9).

There is no wisdom in giving a child material beyond his depth. During the initial period of the Restoration, the Church members were not yet ready to receive those mysteries of godliness involved in the temple ordinances until a firm foundation had first been laid. This point was more fully covered in our chapter on symbols. Let us never forget, moreover, that knowledge carries with it commensurate responsibilities, and that imparting knowledge prematurely may be more catastrophic than advantageous.

The Prophet Joseph Smith did change his position on numerous doctrines, but the word "change" is here used in the sense of "adding to" rather than "contradicting." In the same sense, a third-grade student "changes" his text books when he is promoted to the fourth grade. The gospel edifice was erected, story upon story, each one adding to the one preceding it. The Latter-day Saints not only admit this, but glory in it. In fact, our Ninth Article of Faith makes this principle one of the pillars of our total credo. "We believe all that God has revealed, all that he does now reveal, and that *he will yet reveal many great and important things pertaining to the Kingdom of God.*"

In the Book of Mormon we read the definitive scriptural statement on this subject: "For behold, thus saith the Lord God: I will give unto the children of men line upon line, precept upon precept, here a little and there a little; and blessed are those who hearken unto my precepts, and lend an ear unto my counsel, for they shall learn wisdom; for unto them that receiveth I will give more; and from them that shall say, We have enough, from them shall be taken away even that which they have" (2 Ne. 28:30; see also Isaiah 28:9-13; D&C 98:12).

Finally, in the Doctrine and Covenants, the Lord tells us specifically that "I deign to reveal unto my church things which have been kept hid from before the foundation of the world, things that pertain to the dispensation of the fulness of times" (D&C 124:41).

Temple Construction

The details of the construction of the Nauvoo Temple we shall pass over lightly, though many volumes have been written about it.

The following passage from the *Encyclopedia of Mormonism* will be of interest:

> The Nauvoo Temple, its tower and spire visible from a distance of twenty miles, was the principal structure in the city of Nauvoo. Facing west, it stood on the summit of a gently sloping bluff overlooking the lower part of the city and the Mississippi River. Built from a high-

> quality grayish-white to tan limestone, its imposing walls were erected and finished with great skill. The walls were three feet thick at ground level, with some individual stones weighing as much as 4,000 pounds. . . . The top of the tower stood 158 feet above the ground level, and was graced by a golden statue of an angel flying in a horizontal position (doubtless inspired by the prophecy in Rev. 14:6-7). . . . William Weeks became the official architect and supervised most of the construction. The building was a complexity of architectural styles, yet much of it was also original, inspired by what the Prophet Joseph Smith had seen in a vision. He closely guided Weeks in the design of the temple as he had seen it, requiring for example, that it have round windows on the second level (HC 6:198-197). The call to build so large a structure taxed the resources of a destitute people. The final cost exceeded $1,000,000. Funds came largely from tithes and offerings of Church members, some donating their life savings. Many gave months of physical labor, with little or no remuneration, working from early morning until sundown, even during harsh weather.[36]

What may not be remembered is that the Church in 1840 had a number of stakes outside of Hancock County, Illinois, and Lee County, Iowa (where Nauvoo and Montrose were located, respectively). For example, there was still a strong stake in Kirtland and one in New York City, and in several other metropolitan areas. The reason for our hearing little or nothing about them is that in 1841 a letter went out from headquarters urging all the Saints outside of Hancock and Lee counties to pack up and move to "Zion," which in this case meant Nauvoo and Montrose. The reason given was that all the Church's manpower was needed in order to finish building the temple and other basic structures in Nauvoo. That is an indication of the importance that the Prophet placed on completing the task which the Lord had set before him. By the same token, all the British immigrant-converts were also directed to proceed to Nauvoo. These facts largely explain the remarkably rapid growth of the city during such a comparatively small window of time.

The Temple Construction Continues

It must be mentioned that the sisters also played a conspicuously important role in the temple's construction. Not only did they sew and knit socks, shirts and trousers for the brethren who were doing the manual work, but they were most effective in raising money needed for buying materials and equipment. They started out by assessing themselves the modest sum of one cent per week per person. This sounds like a paltry sum, but they were so zealous in meeting and surpassing this assessment that before it was over they had raised over $2,000 from among themselves, plus considerable amounts from other sources. In a no-frills society, the total amount they raised from all sources was very respectable.

The sisters worked so well together that their resultant bonding created the nucleus for the Relief Society, which was created in March of 1842.

The Saints spared no effort to make the temple the very best one they could. In the revelation of January 19, 1841 (D&C 124:26), they were told to gather their gold and silver and precious stones, and antiquities, and the box-tree, and the fir tree, along with all the precious trees of the earth. These instructions, I suppose, can be viewed as permissible revelatory hyperbole. That is to say, they embody a perfectly understandable exaggeration of the splendor of the temple-to-be in order to emphasize an important point, namely that the Lord expected them to make this temple the most beautiful of which they were capable.

Although history does not record that they ever succeeded in gathering "gold" and "silver" and "precious stones" and the "precious trees of the earth," it does record that they exerted a monumental effort to make this a first-class temple. For example, they sent five expeditions to the "pineries" in Wisconsin to cut timber. The total amount harvested was 995,000 board feet of sawed lumber and 480,000 square feet of rough timber, which they shipped to Nauvoo by binding the logs and boards together to form massive rafts and then floating them down the Mississippi river. Some of this wood went for the construction of the Nauvoo House and other structures, but most of it was destined for the temple. The finished art work and sculpture, both exterior and interior, were superb. The carving out of wood for the baptismal font and the twelve life-size oxen supporting it was an extraordinary achievement in itself.

In considering the over-all performance of these indomitable men and women, the motto of the medieval painter Jan van Eyck comes to mind: "*As I can, but not as I would.*" Van Eyck did his best, and his best, though not measuring up to his own expectations, entitled him a place in history's pantheon of the most celebrated artists. And so the builders of the Nauvoo Temple, though they never succeeded in bringing in the gold and silver and precious jewels and the exotic timber from all over the world, they did succeed in building a very creditable temple, reputed to be the most magnificent building in Illinois and one worthy of divine acceptation.

Further Historical Highlights

On January 19, 1841, the Prophet Joseph Smith received the previously referred-to pivotal revelation identified as Section 124 of the Doctrine and Covenants. Covering ten pages, it becomes the longest revelation in the Doctrine and Covenants. Its salient provisions, as far as temples and temple ordinances are concerned, are as follows. Verses 26 and 27, which have already been commented on, direct the Saints to gather together the treasures of the earth for the construction of a "house to my name."

Verse 28 tells us that the temple will make possible the restoration of that "which he [the Most High] hath taken away, even the fullness of the priesthood." Nothing had been said by the Prophet in his previous revelations or commentaries, up to this point of time, concerning the endowment ceremony as we understand that term today, but this particular verse 28 almost certainly does refer to it. Where the word "endowment" was used previously, it had reference to an outpouring of spiritual strength resulting from temple participation, but was not connected with any particular ordinance.

Verse 28 apparently does refer to a specific ceremony, or ordinance. In the use of the words "fullness of the priesthood" we have a clear foreshadowing of that which was to come, for the endowment ordinance clearly does embody a "fullness of the priesthood" (see also v. 42).

In vv. 29-37 the Lord informs the Saints that they will be given a "sufficient time" to build a "house unto me" [i.e., a temple], and that after the expiration of that time their baptisms for the dead outside the temple would be unacceptable. In fact, if appropriate facilities for performing these sacred baptismal ordinances were not completed within that specified time, then the Saints would be "rejected." As explained above, the Lord's deadline was met by constructing a temporary baptismal font within the time limit.

In v. 38 we learn that the temple will make possible the revealing of ordinances which "had been hid from before the world was." The following verse (39) then lists a number of objectives to be accomplished in the temple, which are "ordained by the ordinance of my holy house." This, and other language in this verse, once again presages the endowment ordinance, the specifics of which were soon to be revealed.

Verse 41, which has likewise already been referred to, tells us that God has revealed to those of this generation things which have never before been given to man. Verses 42-55 elaborate on the theme that those who pollute holy things surrender their right to receive the promised blessings. It is a stark warning, not only to those in charge of the Nauvoo temple, but to all subsequent temples, that whatever is done in a holy temple must only be done by the pure in mind and body. This is probably the genesis of today's practice of requiring a certification of worthiness and purity (i.e., a temple recommend) from all patrons who would enter the temple. In these verses the Prophet is once again instructed to proceed with the construction of the House of the Lord. The Prophet continued for the rest of his life to give emphasis to the importance of the principles enunciated in Section 124 and other comparable revelations.

At a conference held on October 2, 1841, Joseph Smith pointed out the glaring discrepancy in the doctrine which held that where two men, brothers perhaps, were of equal righteousness and integrity, and the one accepted the gospel, and other died without having received that opportunity, the first will be saved and other damned. This doctrine, according to the Prophet, was erroneous. This conviction, which seems so simple and so logical to us, laid the groundwork for the distinctively Latter-day Saint doctrine which holds that those passing beyond the veil without hearing the gospel will have that opportunity in the spirit world.

The minutes taken of the above conference (October 3-5, 1841) presumably quoting the Prophet himself, contain the following: "This doctrine [providing for the salvation of the dead] presents in a clear light the wisdom and mercy of God in preparing an ordinance for the salvation of the dead, being baptized by proxy, their names recorded in heaven and they judged according to the deeds done in the body. This doctrine was the burden of the scriptures. Those saints who neglect it in behalf of their deceased relatives, do it at the peril of their own salvation" (HC 4:426).

These words elaborate a little further the body of doctrine already revealed regarding the salvation of the dead. By this addition we now know that we not only have the right to perform these proxy baptisms, but the *duty* to do so, and, by inference, the duty to search out our ancestors by research, in order to make that possible. If we neglect this duty we do so at the peril of jeopardizing our own salvation.

On November 8, 1841, the baptismal font, now completely enclosed, was dedicated. Two weeks later, the first baptisms for the dead were performed therein. Thus the Lord's instructions, so imperatively given in D&C 124:30-33, were thereby complied with.

The Doctrine of the Endowment

On January 6, 1842, the Prophet made an entry in his journal which indicated that something very wonderful was about to happen. Quoting from it we read:

> Truly this is a day to be long remembered by the Saints of the last days—a day in which the God of heaven has begun to restore the ancient order of His kingdom unto His servants and His people—a day in which all things are concurring to bring about the completion of the fullness of the Gospel, a fullness of the dispensation of dispensations, even the fullness of times; a day in which God has begun to make manifest and set in order in his Church those things which have been, and those things which the ancient prophets and wise men desired to see but died without beholding them; a day in which these things begin to be made manifest, which have been hid from before the foundation of the world, and which Jehovah has promised should be made known in his own due time unto his servants to prepare the earth for the return of his glory. . . .[37]

Now we come to the high point, the event which the Prophet had been waiting for almost from the beginning. Some time between the aforesaid date of January 6 and May 3, 1842, the Lord must have revealed to the Prophet the final and ultimate mystery of the endowment and the sealing ordinances, giving him their details, and the authority to proceed to administer them and to share the keys of administering them with those who would succeed him.

Note carefully the Prophet's entry in his journal, dated May 3, 1842:

> I spent the day in the upper part of the store, that is in my private office (so called because in that room I keep my sacred writings, translate ancient records, and receive revelations) and in my general business office, or lodge room. . . . in council with General James Adams, . . . Patriarch Hyrum Smith, Bishops Newel K. Whitney and George Miller, and President Brigham Young and elders Heber C. Kimball and Willard Richards, instructing them in the principles and order of the Priesthood, attending to washings, anointings, endowments and the communication of keys pertaining to the Aaronic Priesthood and so on to the highest order of the Melchizedek Priesthood, setting forth the order pertaining to the Ancient of Days, and all those plans and principles by which any one is enabled to secure the fullness of those blessings which have been prepared for the Church of the First Born, and come up and abide in the presence of the Elohim in the eternal worlds. In this council was instituted the ancient order of things for the first time in these last days. And the communications I made to this council were things spiritual to be received only by the spiritual minded.[38]

The text of the ceremony was not reduced to writing, of course, because of its sacredness. This point is discussed more fully in Chapter 1. The references herein are to the ordinances which today we call the endowment and sealing ordinances, and with which present-day temple attenders are familiar.

Dr. Truman G. Madsen quotes from the journal of L. John Nuttall. After the brethren referred to above had received their endowment, the Prophet said: "Brother Brigham, this is not arranged right, but we have done the best we could under the circumstances in which we were placed, and I wish you to take this matter in hand, and organize and systematize all these ceremonies." Dr. Madsen, in commenting on the aforesaid, adds: ". . . Brigham Young later said: 'I did so, and each time I got something more. [meaning that each time he worked on systematizing he had not only his memory and the records kept by Wilford Woodruff and others, but also the light of revelation]. So that when we went through the temple at Nauvoo, [without Joseph] I understood and knew how to place them there. We had our ceremonies pretty correct'"[39]

I shall not cite all of the multiple quotations by the associates of the Prophet Joseph Smith (including Brigham Young, John Taylor, Wilford Woodruff, Parley P. Pratt, and others of the Twelve) to the effect that they received their endowment at the hands of Joseph Smith himself, and that the Prophet told them (the Twelve) that he was transferring to them all of the keys, the power, the principles of life and salvation that God had ever given to man who ever lived upon the earth, and that it was up to them to round up their shoulders and to bear off the work of the Kingdom.

These brethren repeated this theme over and over again throughout the rest of their lives, and in all solemnity. These irrefutable facts become the basis of the Church's position today that it is endowed with all the requisite authority to perform the sacred temple ordinances necessary for the exaltation of man. The keys of that enormous authority reside today with the current head of The Church of Jesus Christ of Latter-day Saints, who holds the title and the authority of Prophet, Seer, and Revelator, and President. In addition to the testimonies of the Prophet's associates, enormous amounts of evidence have come to the Church supporting and confirming the fact that the Prophet Joseph Smith did in fact receive from God the authority to administer these Priesthood ordinances of exaltation. He also received the authority to transmit that authority in regular order of succession to his successor, and thence down the line to whomever holds the Presidency of the Church at any particular time, and that the sole authority to administer the affairs of the Kingdom resides in The Church of Jesus Christ of Latter-day Saints, the keys of which authority are held by the President of the Church.

What the record shows is that the endowment and related ceremonies were revealed to the Prophet some time between January 18, 1841 and May 3, 1842. The Prophet Joseph Smith, during the period between May 3, 1842 and his death on June 27, 1844, felt himself to be under a moral compulsion to complete the construction of the temple, to perform the newly revealed temple ordinances for as many worthy members as possible, to communicate to them the essentials pertaining to the administration of the endowment and the sealings, and finally, to give the authority to perform these sacred ordinances to his successors. The official records, as well as the unofficial journal entries, are in substantial agreement on these fundamental points.

On the first and sixth of September 1842, the Prophet wrote two letters, known to us as D&C 127 and 128, respectively. They have been canonized by the Church because the Prophet made it clear that their contents came to him by revelation (D&C 128:2). In section 127 the Prophet requests that a recorder be appointed to act as an eye witness for each baptism for the dead and faithfully record all such baptisms in order that there may be a record in heaven of "whatsoever you bind on earth" or whatsoever you "loose on earth . . ." (D&C 127:6-7).

Section 128 is teeming with information, some of it deeply doctrinal. It should be read by all temple-goers. It ends with a paean of joy and exultation. In it, the Prophet's enthusiasm for the work of administering the saving ordinances for the dead comes gushing forth like a fresh mountain stream, filling its reader with both enthusiasm and wonder.

Refuting the Doctrinal Critics

The above somewhat detailed recitation of the chronological development of the temple doctrines is important because it refutes the contention of those of the Church's detractors who erroneously claim that the doctrines of the endowment, of eternal sealings, and of plural marriage were spurious doctrines, perhaps conceived after the Prophet's death. Because our detractors erroneously feel that therein they have found the Prophet's "Achilles heel," I have deemed it worthwhile to devote a little more space to the issue of the authenticity of Joseph Smith's prophetic calling and the general question of his truthfulness.

Reduced to its simplest formulation, the arguments of our critics are as follows. If they (the critics) accept Joseph Smith's prophetic calling (as does the Reorganized Latter-day Saint Church) then their argument is simply that the Prophet did not say or do the things which the LDS Church ascribes to him regarding the various temple ordinances, but that the latter were pure fantasy, concocted after his death by Brigham Young and his associates. In response, consider the testimonies of the many individuals who were closest to Joseph Smith and received these ordinances at his hands, and who heard him repeatedly declare that they had been revealed to him by Almighty God. These affirmations are consistent with each other and are overwhelmingly persuasive.

If our critics deny the authenticity of Joseph Smith's prophetic calling (and that includes everybody else), their explanation is much simpler, namely, that he did say the things attributed to him, but that he was not telling the truth. The argument assumes that he was driven by an exaggerated ego which led him to form a conspiracy, and, with his co-conspirators, to put together a little empire all his own, populated by thousands of obsequious sycophants who could feed his hunger for celebrity.

This explanation, however, has come into disrepute in later years, even among the Church's critics, because of its non-persuasiveness. It leaves too many vital questions unanswered. Nevertheless, I shall try to respond to it, briefly, for it still has its adherents and because those critics who disagree do not seem to have advanced anything more persuasive. The simple question, then, is whether the Prophet Joseph Smith was telling the truth, not just in Nauvoo, but throughout his adult life.

The premise that Joseph Smith was a liar constitutes a classic example of "begging the question." I use that term as I did in college debate, in the sense of building up an argument based on an assumption which is yet to be proven. In this case, Joseph Smith's non-credibility is based on the assumption that any imaginative, intelligent, but perverse deceiver can fabricate a believable lie. Using that specious assumption as the foundation of its case, its proponents proceed to orchestrate a grandiose attack on the entire story of the Restoration.

Reality, however, shows this assumption to be completely untenable. It is true that even a three-year-old child can tell an irrefutable lie. For example: adult's question: "Does your finger hurt?" Child's answer: "Yes." Such an answer would be easy to fake and impossible to disprove. But as the circumstances become more and more complex, the spinning of a convincing lie becomes more and more difficult, until finally circumstances become so complex as to make any convincing falsification impossible, even for the most brilliant scoundrel.

The anti-Mormon argument seemed to be based on the reasoning that all the Prophet had to do was to decide in his mind to embark on a course of impudent imposture and he could then seduce his gullible followers into accepting his mendacious statements without question. That would not have been possible to do.

All trial attorneys know that it takes a very intelligent witness on the stand in a judicial proceeding to tell a convincing lie, even in a fairly simple factual situation. As the facts grow more complex, it becomes increasingly difficult for him to sustain his position, until finally he finds himself wallowing in so many contradictions that his mendacious charade is exposed and he becomes completely discredited and unbelievable. Why? Because, if, on the one hand, a witness is actually telling the truth, no matter how complex the facts may be, all he has to do is to relate them as he remembers them. He is on safe ground, even under cross-examination. If he doesn't remember, he can say so. But, on the other hand, if he is fabricating a falsehood, then under cross examination he is required to be consistent with every fabricated falsehood expressed on direct examination, which, in a complex set of facts, will be impossible, even for a witness of phenomenal memory. The questions on cross examination will also drag his responses into unfamiliar territory, calling for unrehearsed answers. At that point, he will have no memory-footprints to fall back on to keep him on track. Of necessity he will have to answer extemporaneously. His subsequent answers will then tend to be incoherent and inconsistent with extemporized answers to previous questions, because they will be difficult, if not impossible, to recall.

Now, if we add two more dimensions to the witness's difficulty, it will become even more impossible for him to make his untrue assertions ring true. Suppose that, first, he is asked to testify about a long string of assertions and events going back twenty years before, and, second, about events which hundreds of his confederates have also participated in and about which they are also prepared to testify. He now has both the problem of remembering his false testimony of twenty years ago and everything in between, and also of making his testimony match the testimony of hundreds of other witnesses whose experiences interfaced with his at numerous points. In some cases these other witnesses, let us say, have parted company with him, or are even hostile to him. Any collaboration with them in the preparation of the witness's testimony would therefore be impossible.

Faced with this mnemonic impossibility, the witness's mendacity would be completely exposed, and the jury would conclude that he was a liar. Need I go on? The parallelism between the situation of the above hypothetical witness and that of the Prophet Joseph Smith is readily apparent. For over twenty years the latter involved himself in a tangle of episodes of extraordinary diversity and complexity. Moreover, hundreds of associates shared with him many of his most important experiences. Some of these associates later parted company with him. Some of them even became his adversaries.

Throughout it all, his testimony remained logical, internally consistent, and consistent with the testimonies of his associates concerning their shared experiences, some of which went back many years in time. Significantly, none of his associates, even after the parting of their respective ways, ever claimed that the Prophet had conned them into participating in a massive religious swindle, or of trying to get them to "shave" the truth just a little. Not one person who was present in Kirtland to witness that amazing outpouring of miracles and wonders ever denied that these things happened.

Many of the key events in the whole Restoration story were experienced by the Prophet in the company of one or more other witnesses, such as the restoration of the two priesthoods, the testimony of the three witnesses, the testimony of the eight witnesses, the vision of the three degrees of glory, the appearance of the Savior, Moses, Elias, and Elijah in the Kirtland temple, and many others. For all of these events there were one or more corroborating witnesses and their testimonies matched each other perfectly, making due allowances for inconsequential aberrations resulting from less-than-perfect memories, which are to be expected. In fact, if their testimonies were to match perfectly, this would suggest, not truthfulness, but collusion.

What is significant is that not one of his associates ever accused the Prophet of coming to him in secret and beseeching him not to "spill the beans" regarding these allegedly shared but actually fantasized experiences. Why? For the simple reason that there were no beans to spill. If his alleged shared experiences with hundreds of confederates had been based on an agreed-upon conspiracy of falsification, then, at a later date, he would have been forced to treat those confederates with the utmost finesse, constantly reinforcing their fealty to him with promises of favors in exchanged for perjured testimony.

But that isn't what happened at all! To the contrary, the Prophet castigated all those who merited castigating, including many of his star corroborating witnesses. On some of his most intimate associates he ended up inflicting the ultimate penalty: excommunication. Truth held no terrors for him, for the truth was on his side. In all respects, his conduct was consistent with the conduct of one who was, in fact, what he purported to be, i.e., a prophet who had walked and talked with God.

As we read of the events of the Restoration, including some of the intimate and very personal ones, the fact that strikes us is that the participants—all of them—acted exactly the way we would imagine they would have acted, assuming they were telling the truth. Their actions, as well as their words, clearly consistent with truth.

When we read the story of the lost 116 pages, for example, and of the very visible agony suffered by the Prophet for his serious lapse, and of his mother's pathetic solicitude for his possible fall from grace, and of the mortal terror endured by Martin Harris, almost unto death—for he seriously feared that he had lost his soul—and when we hear his indescribable expressions of ecstasy when he found out that he had been forgiven and was shown the plates as evidence of that fact, our reaction to all this is: "Wow! This story rings true! These people were acting exactly the way imperfect people really do act in that kind of a situation. How does Martin Harris, a farmer, and obviously no thespian, fake a scene portraying himself experiencing such intense emotion, including flowing tears? These were not a cabal of sinister conspirators plotting to perpetrate a monstrous fraud on the world through a heinous deception, but real live, but imperfect, people trying to do their best and acting exactly the way people do act when faced with the unexpected and bitter vagaries, as well as with the ecstasies, of real life. The verdict of the jury, if there had been one, would certainly have been: we believe that the witnesses are telling the truth.

Some contend that the Prophet borrowed the temple ceremonies from the Free Masons. Without having any knowledge of Free Masonry, one can at least make the following observation which, I believe, may have some value. Free Masonry is not a religion, and, *a fortiori,* not a *Christian* religion (although many Masons—perhaps most—are Christians). Many gentlemen of the Jewish faith are also Masons. The Latter-day Saint temple ceremony on the other hand, is both religious and thoroughly Christian. In a sense, it is a celebration of the mission and Atonement of the Savior. To have missed this point is to have failed to understand the whole point of the temple ceremony. Any resemblance between the two ceremonies, therefore, would be very superficial, at most, and not in any way substantive. As previously pointed out, the Latter-day Saint temple ceremonies have some of their roots in ancient Old Testament practices, but, from start to finish, they testify of the divine nature and mission of Jesus Christ.

One final point should be made in this connection. It is customary for biographers of famous achievers to devote a section of their work to discussing the doubts, the uncertainties, the regrets and backward looks of their protagonist. In the biography of Joseph Smith, however, there is no such section, for he had none. This, in itself, would seem to place him in a category all by himself.

Conceding that he never claimed to be perfect and freely admitted his mistakes, and that the Lord on multiple occasions had to reassure him that his sins had been forgiven (D&C 29:3; 60:7; 84:61; and 110:5), and that he readily admitted that "a prophet is a prophet only when he is acting as such,"[40] what is as clear as daylight is that the Prophet Joseph Smith never went through a period of doubts, misgivings, or regrets about the nature of his calling. Pain? Yes. Lots of it. Disappointments? Of course. His life was one long crescendo of disappointments. As one meditates on the terrible grief and agony that must have been torturing his soul while he languished for over five months in that foul, evil-smelling Missouri jail, and as he composed those heroically tragic lines of the 121st and 122nd sections of the Doctrine and Covenants that almost tear one's heart out just to read, one realizes that only a Prophet of God can fully understand disappointment's fullest dimensions. But doubts about his calling? Regretful backward glances? No, not in the least! In all of the millions of words that he spoke and wrote over a twenty-year period—and he kept good records—we do not find one word that suggests that he ever lost his sense of purpose nor the unshakable conviction that he had been called of God, and that the cause to which he was giving his life would ultimately triumph. Anyone who reads the Prophet's biography, if he is honest with himself, will have to be impressed with the fact that he acted exactly like a man should act who verily believed and knew that he had talked to God. It is the testimony of the Latter-day Saints today that he did.

Late Nauvoo Period

The rest of the Nauvoo episode must be covered very briefly. A more detailed account offers some of the most fascinating materials for an attention-riveting drama, but they fall beyond the reaches of this work.

In just a few words, the Prophet continued to urge the Saints to perform proxy baptisms for their dead right up to the moment of his death. He himself performed the endowment ordinances for over eighty members. The Prophet's wife Emma officiated, in the appropriate manner, for the sisters. The Prophet, in the meantime, also taught and trained the Quorum of the Twelve and others to administer the temple endowment and sealing ordinances so that they might be capable of doing so on their own when the proper time should arrive. None of these ordinances were done inside the temple, of course, while the prophet still lived (except baptisms), because the temple was not ready to accommodate them until early in December 1845. Apparently no endowments or sealings for the dead were performed during this Nauvoo period, even after December of 1845, although there were a number of sealings of live spouses to deceased spouses and sealings of children to parents.

On July 12, 1843, the Prophet gave to the Church the revelation on celestial and plural marriage, although the doctrine had been known long before that date. In April of 1844 he delivered his famous King Follett Discourse in which he announced for the first time certain doctrines which were unfamiliar to the Saints, such as the doctrine of the plurality of gods, the progressive nature of God, and the ultimate destiny of the righteous. From this latter concept, President Lorenzo Snow later coined the truism: "As man now is, God once was. As God now is, man may be." These doctrines had been previously foreshadowed, but never put before the world in such a direct and authoritative manner as on that occasion. The Prophet Joseph never had an opportunity to further elaborate upon these profound and very distinctive doctrines, for in two months he was dead.

The Prophet and his brother Hyrum were assassinated on June 27, 1844. Brigham Young and most of the other members of the Twelve were in the east at the time. Sidney Rigdon was in Pittsburgh. From that date until August 8, there was no one generally recognized by the general Church membership to be Joseph Smith's successor, and the Church was literally leaderless.

Events Following the Prophet's Death

Sidney Rigdon arrived in Nauvoo from Pittsburgh on Tuesday, August 6, and began immediately to assert his right to lead the Church, not as a "successor" to the Prophet Joseph (for, he contended, no one could claim that right) but as the Church's "guardian." A general meeting was tentatively scheduled for that very day to give Brother Rigdon an opportunity to present his position. Stake President William Marks, however, postponed the meeting until Thursday, the eighth, at 10:00 a.m. That simple act profoundly changed the course of events.

On the same Tuesday night, Brigham Young and others of the Twelve arrived in Nauvoo and immediately put forward the position that at the death of the Prophet the keys of the kingdom resided uniquely in the Twelve, and not in Sidney Rigdon (D&C 107:24). Meetings were held on Wednesday with the priesthood leaders and the issue was further discussed. On Thursday, August 8, at 10:00 a.m, the meeting previously called by President Marks was held in the grove, attended by a large portion of the entire available church membership.

Sidney Rigdon spoke first for an hour and a half in support of his position. After that, Brigham Young, as president of the Twelve, took the floor and spoke. It was then that, in the eyes of many of those assembled, a physical transformation occurred, which was interpreted by them as a sign from heaven that Brigham Young was to be the priesthood leader of the Church in his capacity as senior member of the Quorum of the Twelve, and therefore the successor to the Prophet Joseph Smith.

The following statement by Wilford Woodruff is typical of the many other statements made to the same effect:

> I was there. The Twelve were there, and a good many others, and all can bear the same testimony. The question might be asked, why was the appearance of Joseph Smith given to Brigham Young? Because here was Sidney Rigdon and other men rising up and claiming to be

> the leaders of the church, and men stood, as it were, on a pivot, not knowing which way to turn; but just as quick as Brigham Young rose in that assembly, his face was that of Joseph Smith—the mantle of Joseph had fallen upon him, the power of God that was upon Joseph Smith was upon him; he had the voice of Joseph, and it was the voice of the shepherd . . . There was a reason for this in the mind of God; it convinced the people.[41]

At 2:00 p.m. the meeting reconvened and President Young again took the floor. This time he announced the principle that the head of the church (in this type of situation) resided with the apostleship. Since the rule of seniority within the Quorum of the Twelve had already been recognized, this meant that the senior apostle, Brigham Young himself, would become the head of the Church, subject to the vote of its members (D&C 107:22). Accordingly, the proposition was put before the assembly and they voted unanimously in support thereof.

Although President Woodruff, in the above quotation, affirmed that the miracle of Brigham Young's transformation "convinced" the congregation, the evidence certainly shows that the sound and inspired logic of President Young's utterances, apart from the miracle, were also enormously persuasive.

What many Latter-day Saints overlook is that President Young was not actually sustained and ordained President of the Church until the 5th of December, 1847, at Kanesville, Iowa. That meant that the brilliant leadership he displayed in personally leading the first company of emigrants to the Salt Lake Valley and in making the historic choice to settle there, was exercised by him in his capacity as president of the quorum of the Twelve Apostles. From the date of the Prophet Joseph Smith's death to the date of President Young's ordination to the office of President approximately three-and-one-half years had expired.

In his new position of authority, President Young began immediately to exercise benevolent but strong and vigorous leadership, which continued until his death in 1877. One must conclude that President Marks must have been inspired to postpone the above proposed meeting of August 6th to the 8th. I feel confident, however, that the Lord would never have allowed his infant church to be deprived of the leadership of the man whom the heavens selected and anointed to this enormously important and historic position of responsibility.

President Young immediately announced a number of policy and administrative decisions which guided the church during the terrifying, yet glorious, years ahead. One of these decisions was that through the tithes of the members, construction work on the temple was to continue until finished. Another policy was that missionary work throughout the world would be intensified. This decision resulted in an enormous influx of foreign converts (especially from Great Britain) to strengthen the still-infant Church.

Construction of the temple continued apace, right up to the moment of its dedication on May 1, 1846, after most of the Saints had already departed. During the period of its construction, however, portions of it were individually dedicated. For example, on November 30, 1845, the top floor alone was dedicated in order to permit endowments and sealings to take place, which they did on the following December 10. The members brought in their own furniture and potted plants for the occasion to embellish the garden and the celestial rooms.

While all this was going on, the black clouds of opposition grew more ominous. Armed guards were posted at the temple's construction site in order to prevent the unfinished structure from being torched by the Church's enemies. The most ominous sign of all, threatening the Nauvoo community and showing how hopeless any further effort would be to amicably settle the differences between the Mormons and their enemies, was the repeal of the Nauvoo charter in January of 1845. This left the city virtually helpless to enforce its own ordinances. There were even threats of the federal government sending federal troops to establish martial law. At that point, it became obvious that the Saints would have to evacuate, and the sooner the better.

Between that date and the date of the final departure, which began on February 15, 1846, the Saints had two preoccupations which preempted all others: finish the temple, and prepare for the exodus. For the Saints, this preparation involved selling their property (usually at a terrible loss) and buying or building the wagons and laying up the store necessary to transport them to points west and allow them to survive.

The top floor of the temple was finally dedicated on November 30, 1845, and the first endowments given on December 10. The first wave of departing emigrants took off on February 15, 1846. So the time intervening between those two dates (sixty-six days) was filled almost entirely by endowing the worthy and qualified members and by making last-minute preparations for the big push. The work schedule followed by the Brethren administering these temple ordinances was almost beyond endurance: eighteen hours a day, six days a week. Although the original date for final departure had been set for February 4, it was postponed to the fifteenth at the last moment to accommodate an additional number of members who had not yet been taken care of. They needed the spiritual strength the endowment could give them to face the ordeals ahead. As previously mentioned, six hundred souls perished in Iowa alone. The number of persons endowed as a result of this frantic last-minute effort totaled about 5,600.

A skeleton crew remained in Nauvoo after the big exodus in February for the purpose of completing the temple's construction and of disposing of the rest of the Church's property. Finally, on May 1 of 1846, the temple was dedicated, but no one was left in Nauvoo to use or enjoy it.

Following its dedication and abandonment, the Saints were spared the embarrassment of having to decide how to dispose of it. As it turned out, there was nothing to dispose of. On November 10, 1848, two incendiaries invaded and torched the building. This so weakened the structure that when a hurricane of unusual force swept through the region a short time later, the demolition was virtually complete, and nothing remained thereafter but a few free-standing monoliths plus piles and piles of rocks. The neighbors and tourists were quick to help themselves to the debris for building purposes, so that eventually there was nothing left whatsoever.

This ended the Nauvoo period, a story of rewards and punishments, triumphs and disasters, joys and sorrows, ecstasies and agonies. As the Saints wended their way westward, they carried with them far more than the stores they had laid up for their physical survival. They had risen high above their suffering and disappointments, from which effort the steel in their character had become refined and tempered. Their ranks had been purged. The fair-weather members had chosen to remain behind. Some had elected to affiliate with one of the various small splinter groups which had formed. In almost every case the latter soon disappeared and deprived their members of the opportunity to play a role in the development of God's great latter-day kingdom.

Those stalwarts who had survived the storms of New York, Ohio, Missouri, and Illinois, and who had endured to the very end were now qualified to establish a new and viable community in the west where none should "come to hurt, or make afraid," and whose members would be strong enough to thrive and expand and to carry a unique message of hope to all the world. None of those wending their way west would ever live long enough to see the Zion they had originally envisioned. But no one, even in all the eternities to come, can ever take away from them the glory and distinction which they earned from having laid the foundation for the Zion which they never saw in the flesh, but which in the due time of the Lord will surely come to pass.

6
Protocol

During my temple presidency I received the following rather astonishing letter:

Dear President King:

As I have visited several temples for proxy work over the years, my feelings have been mixed. Sometimes I have been uplifted, sometimes frightened, and sometimes frustrated. On several occasions I have been nettled by curt instructions from temple workers not to do this and not to do that. Some persons have spoken to me of spiritual experiences and revelations in the Celestial Room. How can I be open to such things if I must anticipate instructions not to sit here, not to talk out loud, and so on. My wife suffers from some nerve deafness, and cannot participate in a whispered conversation. On reaching the Celestial Room the next time, I expect to feel less like lingering than escaping. I speculate that my discomfort might be eased if you were to provide me with a written list of the do's and don'ts so that I might prepare myself in advance to follow that regimen. My bishop claims no knowledge of such a list, but apparently the temple workers know it. Or do they?

Do the temple workers proscribe on their own authority, in which case may I ignore them?

Sincerely,
Anonymous

Having spent several years in politics, I was used to this kind of needling, which, in this case, I suspected was given with the best of intent. In fact, I found my correspondent's candor refreshing. He was saying things which I have felt myself but never had the courage to say. If I had been able to answer my anonymous friend, this is about what I would have said:

Dear Anonymous:

I appreciated your recent letter. If an apology is needed, then I freely offer it. However, not wishing to minimize the importance of what you have said, let me recall for you a little vignette in church history which may be of interest. When Elder Parley P. Pratt of the Quorum of the Twelve complained to the Prophet Joseph Smith that a fellow member of the Twelve had falsely accused him of an improper act, the Prophet simply said: "Brother Parley, just walk these little things under your feet, and carry on the good work."

I frequently tell my temple workers that to optimize their human relations, two "no-no's" must be avoided like poison, viz: "giving offense," and "taking offense," and the second is as deadly as the first. After all, if one never takes offense, there never will be an offense given, or, as the familiar saying goes; "It takes two to tango."

Since I know nothing of the specifics of your unpleasant experience, I willingly accept what you say as correct and express to you both my love and my hope that you will allow nothing to dampen your enthusiasm for continuing to visit the temple. The work is too important to be sidetracked, for any reason.

I willingly acknowledge that temple workers are not perfect angels. They are going through a learning experience, just as you are. In spite of our plea that they be careful not to offend, occasionally they do. I have sometimes said that if a correction cannot be made without creating serious offense, I would rather that the correction not be made at all. I would rather break a rule than break a heart. The official word from Salt Lake is: "Although the Lord is entitled to our very best performance, it would take a very serious mistake, indeed, to totally invalidate an ordinance."

A kind and sensitive way to inform people of the need to follow instructions exists. For some teachers this skill comes naturally, but for others it has to be learned. The latter are the ones referred to by Dr. Truman G. Madsen, who quipped: "Some folks feel that they have been instructed by heaven to draw a line in the sand, and then to spend the rest of their lives making certain that no one ever crosses over it. But this isn't the way the Lord wants us to behave."

In all fairness, however, I should add that examples of unfeeling conduct on the part of present-day ordinance workers are extremely rare. In recent times the Church has had success in getting temple workers to externalize the love that all temple patrons expect. On behalf of those who are still learning to do this, we ask your patience. May you be crowned with heaven's choicest blessings as you continue your good work.

Very sincerely yours,
David S. King

The above letter from Anonymous does raise some unanswered questions, however, which deserve further discussion. One might well wonder, for example, why there should be so many official and unofficial rules prescribing temple conduct that now number in the thousands. These rules fall into a number of categories, but in this chapter we are concerned only with those rules of temple protocol which prescribe personal conduct and worthiness. We exclude those covering the performance and recording of the ordinances themselves, or the operation of the temple.

When I use the word "protocol" I am falling back on the vocabulary of the Foreign Service. In that context, the word protocol refers to those traditions, observances, and customs, written or unwritten, which define what an ambassador should do and should not do in order to run a smooth diplomatic operation without offending or creating misunderstandings or unnecessary international incidents. They are not really laws so much as general understandings which all nations have tacitly agreed to respect. They do so because it is to everybody's advantage.

By the same token, workers and patrons are expected to respect many temple rules of procedure. Many of them have been formalized and written out in rule books. Others have just grown up and are generally accepted because they make sense. Sometimes they, too, find their way into rule books, and sometimes they do not. But they are all intended to accomplish the same thing, and that is to administer the temple ordinances in the way the Lord would have them administered and to do so with such loving care that when the patron leaves the temple he will be spiritually edified, and happy for having come. If these objectives are not reached, then the temple will have failed in its mission.

The Need for Reverence

Some of the above-mentioned rules of "Temple Protocol," if I may borrow the term, have to do with such things as personal attire and adornments, personal cleanliness, special behavior in the celestial and other special rooms, wearing of special temple attire, avoiding controversy, and, above all, maintaining the proper spirit of decorum and of reverence. Speaking only in whispers and meditating upon sacred subjects are also part of temple protocol, whereas frivolity and light-mindedness are frowned upon. Those who feel uncomfortable with these spiritual disciplines are urged to postpone their coming to the temple until they can feel better about complying.

In this connection, the Savior said: ". . . Behold, I am Jesus Christ, the Savior of the world. Treasure these things up in your hearts, and *let the solemnities of eternity rest upon your minds*" (D&C 43:34, emphasis added). If there is ever a place in the world where you can "Let the solemnities of eternity rest upon your minds," that place is a temple of the Lord.

This need for almost total silence can cause concern to some Latter-day Saints and sometimes gives rise to negative reactions, such as those expressed by the writer of the above anonymous letter.

Moreover, everything about the temple is designed to encourage reverence and to discourage unnecessary talking or noise. To this end, every square foot of flooring, from the baptistry all the way to the top floor, is covered with a thick and sound-absorbing carpet. To the same end, the decor of the various sealing and other rooms is subdued and designed to promote quiet reflection.

Notwithstanding the fact that the rules requiring near silence may be difficult for our more talkative patrons to observe, the rules serve a crucial purpose and must remain unchanged. I consider this matter to be of the greatest importance, and this chapter attempts to show why. It goes to the very heart of the temple experience.

A good brother came to me one day and said, in effect: "President King, the temple experience is an extremely happy one for me. It's not like anything else I have ever known. In fact, I am so happy here that I want to shout "Hallelujah" at the top of my voice. But I'm told that I can't do that because the rules require me to go around using a whisper or sign language with which to communicate my thoughts. I don't enjoy wearing this eternal hang-dog expression. What are we trying to do? Turn this temple into a mausoleum?"

In response, I tried to tell him in a nice way that if he thought that being quiet and reverent required exchanging his habitual smile for a perpetual hang-dog expression, he was laboring under a misconception. As a matter of fact, the truly greatest joys in life, I said, were reserved for those who do succeed in understanding the full meaning of the term "reverence."

The fact that some may be less enthusiastic than others about observing the strict rules on reverence and quiet in the temple only confirms what we already know, namely that even within the Church we are all made differently. This is evident from the remarks of my friend who wanted to shout "hallelujah," though others would certainly disagree with him.

Let's plumb this matter a little deeper. It should be noted at the outset that agreeing on the definition and meaning of "reverence" is so difficult because, like other words such as "love," and "light," "reverence" is really indefinable. In order to know what it means, first you have to feel it, and because human beings feel "reverence" in such different ways, their definitions will differ to that degree.

Brother Stephen Covey has made this fact more understandable. In his writings he has given a very specialized definition to the term "paradigm" which he interprets to mean one's total evaluation of a particular reality, which evaluation is a reflection of all the influences which have had any bearing upon its formation, including such things as his genetic makeup, his education and training, his spiritual orientation, his artistic sensitivity, his innate or acquired prejudices, and so on.

Thus, a man will interpret the experience of feeling reverent by viewing it through the prism of his own personal paradigm, which will mark the outer limits of his interpretation of that experience.

Let's take a very simple illustration. In the military cemetery of the United States at Arlington, Virginia, lies the tomb of the unknown soldier. It is reverently guarded by a detachment of select marines dressed in ceremonial uniforms. The lush green backdrop of lawn and trees give it an appropriately natural setting and bespeaks the tranquil and majestic symbolism intended to recall the heroism displayed by countless American soldiers "known but to God," who died on the field of combat.

The site is annually visited by countless tourists. Most of them, *without being told,* have an innate understanding that this is a supremely sacred spot. Small children are told to "hush." Heads are bowed. Voices muted. Tears flow. This is "reverence," felt right to the very core.

And yet there are other tourists who visit the same tomb, and under the same circumstances, but experience no such reaction whatsoever. Their paradigms, or evaluation of this experience, generate no reverence at all. They are unmoved. They go on babbling. They consult their watches. They proceed to the next stop.

I can safely presume that all faithful Latter-day Saints have at least a minimal feeling for the importance of reverence, or they wouldn't be Latter-day Saints. But the diversity of their lives being what it is, there are bound to be differences in the intensity of that feeling. To illustrate that fact, let me change the venue from the Arlington Cemetery to an LDS sacrament meeting which is about to begin. The chapel is filling up with worshippers. An observer could divide them into two groups, based upon the observable differences in their reaction to what is going on.

In the first group the observer will see the typical extroverts. (This does not mean, however, that all extroverts fall into this group, nor that all introverts are excluded from this group.) They are the well-known "people persons." The sacrament meeting affords them an excellent opportunity to greet their friends and to "cheer up the sad and make someone feel glad." Inevitably they fill the chapel with the sounds of their animated conversations.

The occasion also affords this group a fine opportunity to transact their Church business, as most of those persons to be contacted are easily accessible. The meeting will also offer them a golden opportunity to do missionary work. Experience has shown that at the outset, investigators are often more impressed by the love they are shown than by the doctrines they are taught.

In a word, then, the period just before and after sacrament meetings offer the most golden moments for members of this group to put into practice what they conceive to be the very heart and core of the Christian ethic; i.e., expressing love and concern for their neighbors;

in other words, doing exactly what the Savior told them to do. This is what Latter-day Saints are known for all over the world

As is the case in all good things, this friendly socializing is carried on at a price, namely the group's failure to participate in the "spiritual warmup" for the worship service to follow. The beautiful organ prelude music, designed to cause the spiritual juices to flow, is not even heard. The few moments provided for prayerful meditation are spent doing other things.

Now let us look at the second group, which I characterize as the introspective ones, recognizing that this characterization is also an over-simplification.

Those falling into this group have discovered that the greatest unexplored territory accessible to them is not found in the jungles of central Africa, but rather in the depths of their own soul. What they really want is time to explore these depths, and to meditate, to take time to establish their priorities, to renew their commitments, and to commune with God and the infinite. They hunger for the opportunity to escape from the hurly-burly of a materialistic world to find refuge in a sanctuary where they can draw close to God and to their Redeemer Jesus Christ, and to express their love for each of them. They long for a quiet place to purge their minds and souls of all their accumulated cultural clap-trap, to qualify themselves to stand before God, and to hear him speak to them the loving words they long to hear. To them, the sacrament meeting represents an opportunity to accomplish all this.

While the members of group number one are busily engaged in putting Christian principles into practice by fraternizing and shaking hands, the members of the second group are trying to enter into the world of spiritual things and to receive whatever message God has in store for them.

Group number two will good-naturedly chide group one for not being a little more reverent, and group one will good-naturedly chide group two for not being sociable enough. In a sense, both groups are right and are defending worthwhile values, neither of which must be sacrificed. Consequently the Church, as an institution, has never felt that either of these values was expendable. What follows, therefore, must be an attempt to synthesize the two. We have had to shave a little off of each set of values so that they might fit together. The resulting synthesis must be good, as witnessed by the relatively high attendance at our sacrament meetings.

My personal view (which I do not claim to be the "right" view, but only "my" view, or paradigm) is that human beings tend to fall into the error of assuming that all good things are equal or interchangeable. It is often said, for example, that the act of worshiping God embraces every good thing imaginable, including feeding the hungry, clothing the naked, cheering up the sad, bringing consolation to the grieving, and so on. But this stretches the meaning of the word "worship" all out of shape. As praiseworthy as these good things may be, *they do not constitute "worship."* All good things are *not* equal to each other. Worship is man's outward manifestation of his inner relation to God. When the scriptures refer to this relation, it is depicted *in contrast* to his relation to man's fellow men rather than integrated with it. There is no implication that they are equivalent to each other. King Benjamin's famous dictum with which we are familiar, which seems to equate the two, is actually talking about *service* to God and not *worshiping* God (Mosiah 2:17). Thus King Benjamin does glorify the act of serving others, but does not confuse it with paying homage to God.

Note the following typical scriptural passage: "*Thou shalt love* [i.e. worship] *the Lord thy God with all thy heart, and with all thy soul, and with all thy strength, and with all thy mind; and thy neighbor as thyself.*" (Luke 10:27). Note that God is mentioned first. Mankind comes second. Note also that the first of the ten commandments calls for placing the Lord God number one on our list of spiritual priorities and that that primacy is not shared with anyone else (Ex. 20:2-3).

The term "worship" should include, it would seem to me, at least the following concepts: (l) acknowledging faith in God as our Father and Creator and faith in Christ as our Savior; (2) expressing our submission to God's will; (3) expressing thanks for the blessings of mortal life and the assurance of a glorious resurrection; (4) expressing our love for God and acknowledging his love for us; (5) making sacred covenants to abide by God's laws forever; (6) establishing a loving and personal relationship with God; (7) making intercessory supplications on behalf of all those who are in need of God's help; (8) offering prayers for strength to overcome our weaknesses and sorrows; and (9) expressing our resolve to live worthily to enter back into God's presence and to be enfolded in the arms of his love. The list could go on.

In view of the dreadful seriousness of all that is involved in the act of worshiping God, this act should be made the focal point of our sacrament meetings, and nothing else should be allowed to interfere with it. With this in mind, the Church has made great effort in recent years to raise the level of reverence for God in its Sacrament meetings, and this effort has proven effective.

And all of this brings us to the whole point of this discussion on temple protocol. My conclusion is that there is one place in the world where we can always be assured of being able to worship and perform our ordinances of exaltation on the highest possible level of spirituality and reverence, and that is in the House of the Lord. Attending the temple is a win-win experience, in that everybody wins, without compromises or obligatory concessions to conflicting cultural imperatives. There we can all enjoy the experience of worship in its purest form.

The introspective patron, on the one hand, can taste there the sweet quiet ambiance for which he has hungered. Nothing there will mar his spiritual reveries or meditations. Those of the "extrovert" group on the other hand will also find the temple experience rewarding, for in their heart of hearts, they, too, recognize the need to occasionally control their gregariousness in order to concentrate exclusively on the things of the spirit. Even my friend who wanted to shout "hallelujah" eventually became convinced that he needed the refuge of a quiet sanctuary.

For these reasons, the rules comprising temple protocol must never be suppressed nor weakened. *They protect that which makes the temple experience unique*. If they should disappear, then our temple experience would be weakened to that extent. The temple is the most effective refuge in all the world for those whose physical circumstances give them little or no opportunity to find elsewhere the isolation, the quiet, the reverence, and the nourishing bread of life for which their soul hungers.

I must add, however, that these extraordinary results are achieved only by those who prepare themselves to receive them. We draw from a spiritual experience only as much as we have the capacity to receive. If we intentionally squeeze our spiritual receptivity down to the size of a thimble, then by that act we have limited to that tiny quantity the spiritual benefits which will flow to us from our temple experience. Fortunately, however, even this unthinking act will not leave the ordinance without significant value for the deceased for whom the ordinance is performed because of the diminished benefits accruing to the one performing the ordinance.

Protocol and the Rules of Personal Purity

Closely associated with the rules designed to promote greater temple reverence are those establishing inflexible standards of individual purity as a condition for temple participation. Let us discuss them for a moment. The theme of purity in connection with activity in holy places resonates throughout all the ancient scriptures and echoes again in their modern counterpart. In our discussion on "roots," we pointed out that the profanation of a sacred temple was invariably the prelude to its abandonment (as in the case of the Kirtland temple) or to its total destruction (in the case of the Temple of Solomon and the Temple of Herod).

In Section 88 of the Doctrine and Covenants, in which the Lord gave instructions relative to the School of the Prophets and the construction of a Temple, we read:

> And I give unto you, who are the first laborers in this last kingdom, a commandment that you assemble yourselves together; . . . *and sanctify* yourselves; yea, *purify your hearts, and cleanse your hands and your feet before me, that I may make you clean.* (D&C 88:74, emphasis added)

In preparing for the dedication of the Kirtland temple, the Prophet made it clear that only those who had purified themselves, both physically and spiritually, had the right to attend these solemn services. He was influenced, no doubt, by the strong words which the Lord had previously revealed to him: "And inasmuch as my people build a house unto me in the name of the Lord, and do not suffer any unclean thing to come into it, that it be not defiled, my glory shall rest upon it; yea, and my presence shall be there, for I will come into it, and all the pure in heart that shall come into it shall see God. But if it be defiled I will not come into it, and my glory shall not be there; for I will not come into unholy temples" (D&C 97:15-17).

These words are so powerful that they bear re-reading. To the same effect is D&C 94:8-9. In light of the promise of being able to see the Lord in the temple on condition of our purity, how could we do other than make our personal purity a condition to our entering into the temple's sacred precincts?

The rule of the temple, therefore, is that no person can enter it without having first obtained from his or her bishop a recommend, countersigned by a member of the stake presidency. To obtain it, a worthiness interview is first given in which the applicant makes a solemn affirmation of personal purity. The temple doors are shut to those who are not prepared to make such an affirmation.

This strict rule does create some difficulties when its application results in keeping non-member parents from witnessing their son's or daughter's wedding ceremony. Their disappointment is very understandable and must be handled with exquisite finesse and sensitivity. Our basic position, however, cannot be changed. While a Bishop, I had to endure several of these very challenging situations.

I tried to explain that in this connection several things must be remembered. Our temples, unlike our chapels, are not intended for the general public, but for worthy participants in sacred ordinances. Temples are not supposed to be open to all. They are for sanctified men and women who have dedicated themselves to the performance of certain sacred ordinances assigned to them for that purpose. It is true that we do allow guests (in limited numbers) at our sealing ceremonies, but they consist exclusively of persons who have already functioned as participants in the past and have thus qualified themselves to receive the blessings of access to the temple.

Moreover, since the temple ordinances involve activities that are *absolutely confidential*, it becomes impossible to give access to those who have not taken all the steps necessary to qualify themselves to become privy to these confidentialities. Moreover, within the temple there can be no room for miscreants, dissidents, or unbelievers (D&C 97:15-17). Were we to lower the eligibility requirements for admission, inevitably some in that category would take advantage of the lower standards. The temple would thus become host to unworthy occupants and would thereby become defiled. This would incur the risk of having its sacred and precious truths made subject to scorn and contempt. This the Lord cannot permit, and to allow it would subject the party so allowing it to the severest divine censure.

The temple ordinances, by their very nature, can only be administered or participated in by those with faith in the Lord and in the efficacy of the ordinances there performed. The presence of a person totally out of harmony with the things that transpire in the temple would be a contradiction, and contrary to the order of heaven.

Our disappointed non-member mother might argue that she is a strong believer in Christ, that she is personally pure, and that she would never divulge anything that she witnessed inside the temple. But to allow her access to the temple based upon this allegation would throw upon us the impossible burden of passing individual judgment on her and on all others in that category who desired access to the temple.

Under the present system, this judgment of worthiness is made by the applicant's bishop after a minimum of one year from the applicant's having become a member of the Church. Her bishop, during that time, will have had ample opportunity to know from his own observation the degree of her faithfulness. Were we required to pass judgment on complete strangers, the task would become impossible. Moreover, if a non-member applicant were to solemnly affirm that she looked favorably upon the procedures within the temple and would never divulge any of its confidentialities, her failure to become a member of the Church would, in itself, cast doubt on the validity of her affirmation.

The only practicable procedure for us to follow, therefore, is to leave the judgment up to the applicant-patron's bishop, who, according to temple rules, must have known her for at least a year and who, therefore, will know her record of service and devotion to the Church. It would be difficult, almost to the point of impossibility, for a bishop or anyone else to pass reliably sound judgment on a total stranger. As one thinks the problem through it becomes obvious that there is no alternative course preferable to the one currently followed in these matters.

If, for reasons of sentimentality (such as to appease the above non-member mother) or otherwise, we were to allow to enter the temple some miscreant whose purpose it is to subject the temple's sacred procedures to profanation, the consequences would be awesome. "*. . . but if it be defiled, I will not come into it, and my glory shall not be there; for I will not come into unholy temples*" (D&C 97:15-16, emphasis added).

We have now discussed the two major categories of temple rules which fall within the broad category of "Temple protocol": those designed to ensure reverence, and those designed to ensure purity. Most of the multiple individual temple rules can be subsumed under either of these broad categories. For example, within the celestial room there is a rule against kneeling prayers and against reading any kind of written material. This may seem strange, since emphasis is laid on the importance of "prayer" and "learning" within the temple. It was the enforcement of one or both of these rules that apparently piqued the author of the above anonymous letter.

However, their rationale is very simple to understand. The celestial room may on occasion hold a hundred people. If half of them were on their knees facing in different directions, and each one offered his or her individual and supposedly private prayer, these prayers would cease to be individual or private. One wonders whether this spectacle might not risk becoming, in some cases, the exhibitionism deprecated by the Savior (see Matt. 6:6-7). Moreover, it would certainly create undesirable confusion for those not praying. Patrons *are* encouraged to pray in the temple, for the latter *is* a house of prayer (D &C 109:8). But prayers do not have to be offered on one's knees. In the Celestial Room one can very easily sit in silence, and with eyes closed, offer up as sincere a prayer as would be possible anywhere else.

As for forbidding the "reading" of written material in the celestial room, again, the logic is plain and convincing. The Church does not wish to convert the temple into a library, and permitting promiscuous reading and studying (which would invite the use of writing materials) in the temple's main room, would run the risk of doing so. The patron's attention should always focus on the temple ordinances themselves and not on studying from books. Moreover, if the patron were to be reading in the celestial room, it would indicate that he had been carrying these materials with him before reaching it, which, in itself, would prove to have been both an inconvenience and a distraction, incompatible with the single-mindedness which should characterize the performance of the ordinance.

It should also be noted that scriptures are provided at convenient places in the temple for patron-use where the circumstances are deemed appropriate.

I deem it unnecessary to pursue any further analysis of individual rules. Suffice it to say that they have been conceived after long and prayerful consideration and practice, and are deemed to be wise and appropriate. Their purpose is to make the temple a fit place to receive the exquisite blessings to which all temple-goers are entitled.

7
Redemption of the Living and the Dead

The Reality of the After-Life

Of all the unresolved mysteries to torment the minds of men, the one most often belabored by sermons, dramas, folk tales, novels and myths is the mystery of death. This should come as no surprise, for everyone knows that nature has pronounced upon every baby born into the world the sentence of death. Only the date is unknown. Nor is it surprising that wild and untamed fantasies about what happens after death should have produced such a number of unholy offspring, such as necromancy, voodoo, witchcraft, and even demon worship. Preoccupation with death is part of the universal human psyche, and it grows out of the longing of the human heart to find out the answer to life's ultimate question: what happens to me when I die?

> The fear of death, that undiscovered country from whose bourne no traveler returns, puzzles the will, and makes us rather bear the ills we have than fly to others that we know not of.
>
> From Shakespeare's *Hamlet*

The subject of death has even become the object of scientific investigation, since a few respected scientists have now become part of the act. The reader may, perhaps, remember a trilogy of books which appeared not too long ago written by Dr. Raymond A. Moody, and entitled "Life After Life," "Reflections on Life After Life," and "Light Beyond." Dr. Moody is a reputable physician as well as a licensed psychiatrist, thus combining expertise in the practice of healing both mind and body. Halfway through his career he began to take seriously the fact that a number of his patients had told him that they had had an out-of-body experience in which their spirits had left their bodies at the moment of dying, often during an operation. After lingering in space for an indeterminate period of time, their spirits had returned to their bodies. During this interim, their spirits, freed from bodily constraints, could actually turn around and watch the physicians operating on their own body. Dr Moody decided to write a book on the subject, which later became three books. These books reported to the world the results of over a thousand individual interviews given to various patients—some not his own—who claimed to have had an out-of-body experience. These experiences were not characterized by Dr. Moody as "after death" (or more accurately "after dying"), but "out of body experiences," however, out of deference to those inveterate skeptics in his own profession who claimed that he could not scientifically prove that the patients had actually died, even though the clinical evidence was overwhelming that they had.

Other men and women of science have also written similar books. Without exception those interviewed by Dr. Moody, and others, testified that: (1) they believed their experience to have occurred after they died; (2) during the experience they retained full consciousness, and in many cases, acquired new information that they had not had before dying ; (3) the after-dying experience was so different from their own mortal life experience that they had no words to adequately describe it; and (4) it was so wonderful, and so filled with light, love, and forgiveness that death thereafter held no terrors for them whatsoever. One woman, when asked how she felt about dying again, simply answered "I can't wait."

One of the most challenging and complete books on this subject, written by Duane S. Crowther, and written from the LDS point of view, is entitled *Life Everlasting*.[42] It preceded the works of Dr. Moody, and still is available as a respected Latter-day Saint "classic."

These experiences are referred to here, but not to "prove" the existence of an after-life. The Latter-day Saint doctrine on the subject is so strong and convincing that this type of proof is not needed, and it is always possible that out of such a wide spectrum of witnesses, some of them may prove to have been suspect. However, these accounts have a certain usefulness because they furnish new insights on the subject, and also give food for thought to those in the world who are still searching for an anchor to their faith.

I use the subject of dying as an introduction to my discussion of the Latter-day Saints' understanding of the redemption of the dead because of its importance to most people. It has always caused me to wonder why today's popular newspapers and magazines do not devote more space to critiquing the whole subject of man's belief in the hereafter.

Apparently for reasons of their own, some popular media have stamped the subject of death as "untouchable." I am not referring, of course, to their distasteful sensationalizing of death as an "event." That, we can do without. What I believe the public would appreciate is receiving more intelligent discussions on how one's belief in an after-life impacts on his attitude toward his present life and on his ability to face death with equanimity. The inevitable consequence of shying away from the subject is that too often it is either ignored or trivialized.

Many of today's psychiatrists and other healers of mental aberrations also tend to stay clear of any discussion of the afterlife, perhaps failing to realize how important the subject is to many of their patients who really do believe in an afterlife. Though there are many exceptions to this, it may be that they are strengthened in their position by the flood of "out-of-body" experiences which, as mentioned above, are being reported with greater frequency.

Many professional care-givers have already learned the value of bringing these sensitive issues into their discussions with their sick or dying patients. I believe the indisputable facts are that, to many of their patients, reassurance of an after-life is very important in achieving the mental comfort to which they are entitled.

Facing the Reality of the After-life

Showing interest in one's life hereafter is certainly not "morbid," as some contend—at least not to those who have an assurance that there is a life hereafter and that it is glorious to those whose mortal life has prepared them for it. It is the same kind of exhilaration that one feels in planning a wonderful trip to some faraway place, only much more so. The subject is morbid only to those for whom dying is like stepping off into a black void.

There are those who insist that we shouldn't waste our time concerning ourselves about such enigmatic matters, but rather should concentrate on the immediate problems of the day. Typically, I have heard it expressed as follows: "I'll leave it up to God (if there is a God) to take care of me when I die, but for the moment, I am not going to worry about it."

I agree that such advice might be good for one who has absolutely no clue as to what the future holds for him, and no desire to find out. It is poor advice, however, for one who does have knowledge of the reality of the hereafter and of the present need to prepare for it.

When my family takes an extended trip, we *do* take time to obtain proper road maps, hotel information, guide books, and the like. Otherwise, our trip could turn into a pure horror of scrambled itineraries and detours, inadequate accommodations, and other disappointments that prior planning could have avoided.

The facts of life are that human beings *do* live each day in the shadow of tomorrow, and are profoundly affected by it. That is the only way they *can* live. As teenagers we plan for a college career, and woe unto those who want one but who don't plan to make it possible. As young adults we plan for marriage and family. We plan for our professional careers, we plan for our vacations, we plan for our retirement. In fact, we plan for almost everything we do. This is not only not wrong, but it is a requirement for survival.

Moreover, Latter-day Saints have been allowed to see their mortal lives in the larger context of both their pre-mortal existence and its continuation after death, stretching on into infinity. Just as the effect of people's actions in their pre-existence carries over into their mortal life, so their actions in mortality will carry over into the hereafter. Would it not be ill-advised on their part, therefore, to refuse to take advantage of this vision of life in its enlarged context, by making long-range plans accordingly? Latter-day Saints look forward to what lies ahead, not with morbidity, but with joyful anticipation.

For Latter-day Saints, dying is comparable to passing from one room into another and more beautiful room. One of our modern scriptures reads: "And it shall come to pass that those that die in me shall not taste of death, for it shall be sweet unto them" (D&C 42:46). The Prophet Joseph Smith had this to say on the subject: "All men know that they must die. And it is important that we should understand . . .

our departure hence . . . It is but reasonable to suppose that God would reveal something in reference to the matter, and it is a subject we ought to study more than any other. We ought to study it day and night, for the world is ignorant in reference to their true condition and relation. If we have any claim on our Heavenly Father for anything, it is for knowledge on this important subject"[43]

Salvation Is Available to All

Latter-day Saints view God's relation to his children as that of a Father in whose image and likeness they are created, and whose love for *all* of them is beyond comprehension. It follows that this infinite love should extend, not just to those of his children who lived in a close speaking relation with him (such as in both Old and New Testament times), but even to those of his children who have never heard of him.

Latter-day Saints view God's children—all of them, stretching out to all ages of time, and space, and stations in life—as one mighty family, united by their common divine parentage. For us, achieving the goal of entering back into the presence of God is both unilateral and multilateral. I use the term unilateral in the sense that each child of God will be judged on the basis of his own faith and works and cannot ride to glory in someone else's chariot of fire. But it is also multilateral in the sense that God has placed on his children the responsibility of doing for others certain things which the latter were not able to do for themselves. Each one will be judged on the basis of what he did for others, as well as on what he did for himself. Just one example of this principle: Every person on earth must receive certain ordinances as a condition to his or her entering into the presence of God (exceptions being made for those who die as infants). Many, however, lived at a particular period of time in human history when those ordinances were not available. For example, baptism by immersion for the remission of sins is an ordinance which could not have been performed when the requisite authority to perform that ordinance was not present on earth.

Out of this principle has grown the Latter-day Saint doctrine of doing vicarious work for the dead: that is, performing certain ordinances by a living person for and in behalf of one who is deceased. This vicarious act, if done by one having authority, in a temple, will be effective both on earth and in heaven, on condition that the person in whose behalf it is performed accepts, while in the spirit world, the act performed in his behalf. He has the perfect right, of course, to reject it if he so desires.

The Lord has not asked anyone to do anything affecting his eternal salvation for which the means of accomplishing it are not also provided.

The Atonement

An important word of explanation is appropriate here in order to complete the picture. The principle of the Atonement of Jesus Christ is the most important of all principles relating to man's eventual exaltation. The above statement that man's exaltation depends upon his own faith and works is accurate only to the extent that it applies to those acts for which he will be held responsible. But Latter-day Saints fully recognize that man, by himself, regardless of his strong faith and good works, is totally incapable of wiping away the effects of the original sin of our first parents, or of his own individual sins, or of transforming mortality into immortality, without the intervention of the infinite atonement of Jesus Christ. The grace of God, when the term is used in this context, means God's doing for man what man is incapable of doing for himself. Grace is unearned. It is more than a *quid pro quo* [this for that]. It is an expression of the pure love of Christ. It is a gift made available to saints and sinners alike. It is the keystone in the arch of Latter-day Saint soteriology [the doctrine of salvation through Jesus Christ].

The result of that Atonement is that the sentence of spiritual death, i.e., estrangement from God resulting from the fall, will be revoked, and physical death will give way to *a universal resurrection for all of God's children.* In addition, individual sins (including mistakes), will be forgiven and exaltation assured on condition that the sinner accept the Savior's redeeming sacrifice, that he sincerely repent of his sins, that he obey God's commandments, and that he receive (or have performed vicariously) the necessary gospel ordinances, some of which can only be performed in a holy temple.

Those who choose to do all of the above become worthy to receive the highest degree of glory, which Latter-day Saints refer to as the Celestial Kingdom. Those who, through the exercise of their free agency elect to do less than the above, will receive a lesser glory, which in the judgment of God will match the state they find themselves in, after they fail to do all that was within their power to do.

The Principles of Exaltation

Basic to the above scheme of things is the principle that all of God's children will be given an opportunity, through the exercise of their free agency, to conform to gospel requirements.

This is made possible by the fact that the gospel of salvation will be preached to all those who have passed into the spirit world without having had a chance to hear it adequately preached to them in mortality. They will be given that opportunity *in the spirit world.* Their death does not write the final chapter in the earthly struggle to earn a heavenly reward. This means that the door still remains open for all, after death, to further improve their relations with God and to further expand their knowledge. It means that the results of all of the cruel inequities and random caprices of life can be rectified in the hereafter. In other words, mankind's final judgment will be absolutely fair and just for all, not dependent on whether individuals were born in a particular place or at a particular time in history. All will be dealt with according to the rules and principles of justice.

The innate sense of justice within us tells us that the final judgments by which we are to be judged should make allowance for human error, and that the possibility of repenting and being forgiven should not be cut off forever at death. At the very least, each person born into mortality should be given a fair chance to rectify those of his deficiencies which are the result of his being human, particularly the result of the unfavorable circumstances which surrounded him during his life. We know that eternity's final playing fields will be level, but this life's playing fields are grotesquely bumpy. Any plan of salvation which fails to recognize this fact does not meet the minimum standards of fairness and justice which the God whom we worship has told us are among his eternal attributes.

This principle of giving to all men and women an equal opportunity to hear the gospel preached to them in the spirit world and of having the necessary ordinances performed for them on earth by proxy is profoundly significant. It removes the apparent inequity inherent in the instruction of the Savior to his disciples to preach the good news to all the world (Mark 16:16), which carries with it the erroneous implication that those who do not accept it (in the flesh) will be damned.

Much more could be said about the doctrine of the Atonement and the debt we owe to Christ for freeing us from the burden of our individual sins, as above explained. It is the most important of all the gospel principles.

An eminent LDS scholar expressed it in these words:

> Nothing in the entire plan of salvation compares in any way in importance with that most transcendent of all events, the atoning sacrifice of our Lord. It is the most important single thing that has ever occurred in the entire history of created things; it is the rock foundation upon which the gospel and all other things rest. . . .[44]

However a further exploration of these principles carries us beyond the purview of this chapter, which deals with the right of all those who have ever lived on the earth to enjoy the same privileges of hearing and accepting the plan of salvation.

What Happens at Death?

Returning, now, to the question asked at the outset: what does happen to us when we die? The position of the LDS Church is that the human spirit retains its existence and separate identity forever. It existed before coming to earth and will continue, after death, into the eternities. At death the spirit enters into a realm where a separation is made between the wicked and the righteous. In the latter category a further distinction is apparently made between those righteous who died having heard and accepted the gospel and those righteous who had not. Presumably this is done to facilitate the latters' receiving the gospel through the proselyting done by the former. In this connection, see D&C 138:12-19, 57.

As mentioned above, we are told in D&C 42:46 that death will be "sweet" unto those who die in the Lord.

In Section 19 of the Doctrine and Covenants we are informed that the words "eternal punishment" which appear rather frequently in sacred scriptures do not, in themselves, indicate that any particular individual will be eternally punished, but only that the principle of punishment for sins is an eternal principle. This is comforting, and confirms the fact that repentance is an eternal principle.

Now, turning to Alma 40:11-13:

> Now, concerning the state of the soul between death and the resurrection—Behold, it has been made known unto me by an angel, that the spirits of all men, as soon as they are departed from that mortal body, yea, the spirits of all men, whether they be good or evil, are taken home to that God who gave them life. And then it shall it come to pass, that the spirits of those that are righteous are received into a state of happiness, which is called paradise, a state of rest, a state of peace, where they shall rest from all their troubles and from all care, and sorrow. And then shall it come to pass, that the spirits of the wicked, yea, who are evil—for behold, they have no part nor portion of the Spirit of the Lord; for behold, they chose evil works rather than good; therefore the spirit of the devil did enter into them, and take possession of their house—and these shall be cast out into outer darkness.

The above scripture raises questions. For example, when the righteous die, do they go immediately into God's presence? The answer is no. President Joseph Fielding Smith makes this very clear: "'Taken home to God' simply means that their mortal existence has come to an end, and they have returned to the world of spirits, where they are assigned to a place according to their works, with the just or the unjust, there to await the resurrection."[45] Another question: does that passage mean that those that are cast into outer darkness remain in outer darkness for all eternity? Again, the answer is no. Again we turn to President Joseph Fielding Smith, who, in answering that question, quotes from D&C 76:106:

> 'These are they who are cast down to hell and suffer the wrath of Almighty God, until the fullness of times, when Christ shall have subdued all enemies under his feet, and shall have perfected his work.' [He then comments as follows]: Yet these, after they have been punished for their sins and after having been turned over to the torments of Satan, shall eventually come forth, after the millennium to receive the telestial kingdom [referring to Doctrine and Covenants 76:111-112.][46]

Section 137 of the Doctrine and Covenants gives us further insights upon the subject. A fuller account of it was given in chapter 4. The Prophet received a vision of the Celestial Kingdom while he and his father and other church dignitaries were with him in the not-yet-dedicated Kirtland temple. He saw his deceased brother Alvin, a righteous young man, who had died before having had an opportunity to receive the gospel and be baptized.

It was then made known to the Prophet that Alvin was an "heir" to the Celestial Kingdom of God, because he was of a disposition to have received and accepted the gospel if he had lived. The point of the revelation, as far as we are here concerned, is that Alvin was not, at that moment, actually in the Celestial Kingdom, but was only an heir thereto. In the civil law, heirs to a testator's estate do not yet have full, vested rights, for certain things first to have occured, such as the death of the testator. Until then, their rights are only inchoate. And so with Alvin and all others in his category. As heirs to the Celestial Kingdom, their rights will become vested (i.e., locked into place) only after certain pre-conditions are satisfied, namely the performance of the temple ordinances of exaltation.

Finally we come to the famous Section 138 of the Doctrine and Covenants, given to President Joseph F. Smith, the sixth president of the Church, six weeks before his death in October 1918. This scripture gives us more specific information about what happens to us when we die than any other scripture, ancient or modern. This revelation tells us (as previously mentioned) that in the spirit world the line of demarcation is drawn between the wicked and the righteous. On the righteous side of the line another line of demarcation is also drawn separating those who lived righteously, but who had not yet received a fullness of the gospel, from those who both lived righteously and who had received a fullness of the gospel.

It was also made known that while the Savior's body lay in the tomb his spirit visited the spirit world, where he accomplished two things: first he commenced the work of preaching to those righteous who were ready to receive the gospel, and, second, he also inaugurated the work of preaching to the wicked. He did not visit the wicked, personally, however, but organized those who would later go forth to preach to them.

With regard to the above-cited passage in Alma, the further question might be asked: after the wicked repent and receive the gospel as preached to them in the spirit world, do they become "heirs of salvation?" The following verses from Section 138 answer that question in the affirmative:

> I beheld that the faithful elders of this dispensation, when they depart from mortal life, continue their labors in the preaching of the gospel of repentance and redemption, through the sacrifice of the Only Begotten Son of God, among those who are in darkness and under the bondage of sin in the great world of the spirits of the dead.
>
> The dead who repent will be redeemed, through obedience to the ordinances of the house of God, and after they have paid the penalty of their transgressions, and are washed clean, shall receive a reward according to their works, for they are heirs of salvation (D&C 138:57-59).

These impressive doctrines are clearly foreshadowed in the following biblical passages: Isaiah 61:1-2; Luke 4:18-19; John 5:25; 1 Pet. 3:18-20; 4:6, etc. Baptism for the dead is inferentially verified in 1 Cor. 15:29.

In the early days of temple work for the dead by proxy, ordinances were performed only for those whose names were found in one's direct ancestral line and who were deemed worthy to receive them. Later the scope was broadened to include all those whose names appeared in one's ancestral line, regardless of their presumed worthiness. Today, all limitations are removed, and there is now no requirement that there be established a genealogical connection between the deceased and the one performing the ordinance in his behalf, nor is there any effort to screen out the unworthy.

Members are still given the special responsibility, however, to perform temple work for those appearing in their own ancestral line. For failure to do this, they will be held responsible.

The ultimate goal of the Church is to perform the ordinances of exaltation for every person who has ever lived, save those who are known to have died in their infancy, for whom sealings alone are required. We must vigorously pursue our family history research back in time until we have gone as far as possible, researching all branches of the family.

At that point, we presume that the Lord will step in to help us, but not until we have done all that we can do (2 Ne. 25:23).

We must be everlastingly grateful to the Lord for giving us, through modern revelation, far more light on the subject of the redemption of the dead than is available in our present Bible.

In Chapter 5, the development of the distinctive doctrine of vicarious work for the dead is briefly traced, and will not be repeated here. This much must be added, however, to make the discussion more complete. As we know, the Angel Moroni appeared to the Prophet Joseph Smith during the night of September 21-22, 1823. Among other things, he quoted from Malachi 4:5-6 (with significant changes from the original), as follows:

> Behold, I will reveal unto you the Priesthood, by the hand of Elijah the prophet, before the coming of the great and dreadful day of the Lord. And he shall plant in the hearts of the children the promises made to the fathers, and the hearts of the children shall turn to their fathers. If it were not so, the whole earth would be utterly wasted at his coming.[47]

What do these words mean? They mean, among other things, that in the latter days a great surge of genealogical research will take place whereby those of this generation will be driven to find out more about their ancestors and to establish their ancestral lines. This strong impulse will extend even to those who are uninformed in the gospel principles, but who would thus be, through their research efforts, unwittingly fulfilling Malachi's prophecy and facilitating and hastening the great latter-day vicarious work performed by faithful members on behalf of their departed dead.

Little imagination is required to project one's interpretation of those two verses to include the concept that in the spirit world great numbers of spirits were assigned to come to earth during an unfavorable period of human history, i.e., a period when the gospel was not on the earth. At that time it was promised to them that if they came, they would not suffer eternally and be deprived of the opportunity to hear the gospel preached to them in the flesh, or of receiving the ordinances necessary for exaltation. Further, they were promised if they were to lay the necessary foundation for the work which was to follow them (for example to establish a free land in which the gospel seed could take root and flourish), the gospel would be preached to them in the spirit world and the necessary ordinances of exaltation performed for them by their (hopefully) grateful posterity.

This, very possibly, is what was meant by "the hearts of the children shall be turned to their fathers."

The pivotal event in the unfolding of the doctrine of vicarious work for the dead was the appearance of the Prophet Elijah to the Prophet Joseph Smith and his companion Oliver Cowdery in the Kirtland temple one week following its dedication. These two men had retired to the west segment of the temple's large assembly room, and had dropped the curtain, thus shutting them off from the rest of the room, assuring their privacy.

The following is the sequence of events which occurred in answer to their fervent prayer. First, the Savior of mankind appeared and accepted the temple, with the fateful words: "For behold, I have accepted this house, and my name shall be here; and I will manifest myself to my people in mercy in this house. Yea, I will appear unto my servants, and speak unto them with mine own voice, if my people will keep my commandments, and do not pollute this holy house" (D&C 110:7, 8).

Following that, Moses appeared, and committed the keys of the gathering of Israel from the four parts of the earth and the leading of the ten tribes from the land of the north.

Then Elias appeared and committed the dispensation of the gospel of Abraham, saying that "In us and our seed all generations after us should be blessed." Finally, the prophet Elijah appeared for whose return the world had been waiting for over two millennia.

Here is the text recounting this great event:

> After this vision had closed, another great and glorious vision burst upon us; for Elijah the prophet, who was taken to heaven without tasting death, stood before us, and said: Behold the time has fully come, which was spoken of by the mouth of Malachi—testifying that he [Elijah] should be sent, before the great and dreadful day of the Lord come—to turn the hearts of the fathers to the children, and the children to the fathers, lest the whole earth be smitten with a curse—Therefore,

> the keys of this dispensation are committed into your hands; and by this you may know that the great and dreadful day of the Lord is near, even at the doors (D&C 110:13-16).

When the prophet Elijah said, "Therefore the keys of this dispensation are committed into your hands" what dispensation was he referring to? Obviously he was referring to that which he had just talked about in the preceding sentence, that is, "turning the hearts of the fathers to the children, and the children to the fathers." In other words, Elijah was thereby conferring on the Prophet Joseph Smith and his designees and successors the authority and keys to carry out the entire program which we call today "temple work," that is, the work of performing ordinances of exaltation on behalf of all for whom such ordinances had not been performed while in the flesh.

The program is predicated on three principles, namely: (1) certain earthly ordinances are necessary to achieve exaltation; (2) these ordinances may be performed for any deceased person by proxy, in the proper way, by any qualified living person, and (3) the person receiving the ordinance by proxy is free to accept or to reject it.

The dimensions of this program, which points to the possible exaltation of untold billions of souls who have departed this life, and which also involves the efforts of millions of faithful Saints while in the flesh to make these ordinances possible, are staggering beyond the power of our imagination. In my humble opinion, there is no possibility that Joseph Smith, that "unschooled frontiersman," as brilliant as he was, could have composed a philosophy and plan for the salvation of the human race of such scope, nobility, and grandeur, without God's direct help and approval. I so testify with all my heart.

8
Preparing for the Temple

Referring to the blessings to come to those who faithfully fulfill their temple responsibilities, Elder Boyd K. Packer said:

> When you come to the temple and receive your endowment, and kneel at the altar and are sealed, you can live an ordinary life and be an ordinary soul—struggling against temptation, failing and repenting, and failing again and repenting, but always determined to keep your covenants. . . . Then the day will come when you will receive the benediction: "Well done, thou good and faithful servant: thou hast been faithful over a few things, I will make thee ruler over many things: enter thou into the joy of thy Lord."[48]

And so the General Authorities have sounded a call to the temple, where unbelievable blessings await you. This chapter is designed to give you a little more information on how to get there and what to do when you arrive.

Three warnings come with it, however. First, this information represents only a thimbleful of all that you eventually will want to know.

Second, regardless of what is said in this chapter, check with the appropriate authorities before making important temple decisions. Although fundamental temple principles remain permanent through the years, inevitably temple procedures are updated and adapted to local conditions, necessitated by differences in the size of the temple, or by other variables, of which the patron should be aware.

The third warning is to not expect to receive answers to all of your questions. As explained in Chapter One of this book, much of what transpires in the temple is highly confidential and is not to be discussed, even inside the temple. Moreover, many questions remain to which the Lord has not yet favored us with authoritative answers.

Information on Temple Procedures

If you are an own-endowment patron, your bishop will be able to help you to become properly oriented and will also organize a Temple Preparation course for you. This will involve both a competent instructor plus a manual containing much necessary information. It is also advisable for you to attend a Temple Orientation Class which involves only one session given under the direction of the stake president, and which utilizes a Temple Media Guide.

Let me stress another point in this connection. You don't have to have any computer savvy or be in possession of any proxy names before accessing the temple. As far as having a proxy name is concerned, on your first visit to the temple the only name you will need is your own. Afterwards, the temple will simply reach down into its "temple file," a pool of countless names of individuals unknown to you, and pull out one for you to use. The angels in heaven will rejoice just as much over what you do for that unknown individual as they will over what you do for your own great-grandfather. The point is that you don't have to let the lack of a proxy name to process, or your unfamiliarity with family history procedures or computers, deter you from going to the temple. If you are worthy of a recommend, you may start immediately.

The temple really does an excellent job of taking care of and briefing its own-endowment patrons. When you arrive in the temple, you will be given an escort who will accompany you throughout all phases of the endowment, including the initiatory ordinances. He or she may also be able to answer some of your more private questions. Moreover, you may bring your own escort with you, if you wish. In addition, one of the regular temple ordinance workers will be on hand, upon your arrival, to show you exactly what to do at each step of the way. And finally, as a climax to your introductory instruction, a member of the temple presidency will give you a lecture, highlighting the things you need to know before assuming the responsibilities of the endowment. Moreover, the endowment ordinance itself will be essentially self-explanatory, at least with regard to those things which you need to know. With all of the above-named resources at your command, you will receive a solid foundation of knowledge of temple procedures. Of course, you will eventually forget a lot of it, but the nice thing about the system is that you can keep coming back again and again to refresh your memory.

If an advance request is made for language interpretation facilities, they can almost always be regularly provided. If not, some other special arrangement can usually be made. The general rule is that every worthy person is entitled to receive his or her temple ordinances, and if linguistic or physical impediments exist, some means will be devised to circumvent the difficulty. For the deaf, for the blind, for the lame, and for the feeble, the temple administrators will always be ready to work things out. If it means bringing in a helpless patron on a stretcher, then so be it. Thus, *no one* with a valid recommend will be turned away from the temple because of personal limitations.

Even those suffering developmental retardation have not been overlooked. The Lord has brought them, in a very special way, into the arms of his love. Special rules have been approved for their benefit, and the temple authorities can supply you with details.

In my opinion, the most important thing for you to know if you are approaching the temple experience for the first time is that you will be asked to make some very important covenants with the Lord regarding the way you conduct your life thereafter. These covenants are so important that you will be held accountable to the Lord for their violation. How will you know, then, whether you want to enter into such covenants without first knowing what you are getting into? The answer is very simple. If you believe that God, who loves you, will never ask you to do anything that is not for your own best good, then you should have no problem. These covenants are for your own best good, in many wondrous ways.

Among other things, you will be asked to wear a temple garment, which is a form of underclothing, for the rest of your life, subject to certain conditions. The marvelous blessings accompanying this practice will be fully explained to you. They make sense. The best explanation of them, in my opinion, is given by Elder Boyd K. Packer, in his splendid book *The Holy Temple*.[49] I recommend this book for everyone.

Every ward or branch in the world is located within a specified temple district. Worthy members are free to attend any temple, wherever located, but are particularly urged to attend the one in whose district they reside. The proliferation of temples throughout the world has made access to them progressively easier.

Members are urged to set their own temple attendance goals, and then to try to meet them. Almost every "How to Succeed" book ever written contains a section on "make your goals specific." We all recognize that good intentions are not enough, and whether we are dealing with success in the things of the world or the things of the Spirit, the rule is the same, namely: until these good intentions are translated into a specific action-program, they will soon evaporate and disappear. Therefore, temple dates must be marked off on the calendar, and action taken when those dates arrive. They should be looked forward to with joyful anticipation.

However, it is not proper for those in authority, at any level, to fix temple performance "quotas" for any individual or group, nor to require from such individual or group an accounting of the amount of temple work accomplished. Motivation should come from a personal desire, internally generated, rather than from the disciplines externally required to meet a prescribed quota.

The wisdom of Elder Glen L. Pace in this regard, quoted in the General Conference Report of 1986, is pertinent: "Programs blindly followed bring us to a discipline of doing good, but principles properly understood and practiced bring us to a disposition to do good."

Types of Recommends

For access to the temple, any member who is eight years of age or over, must have either one, or under the circumstances mentioned below, two, of the following three kinds of temple recommends:

1. ***Temple Recommend.*** This is the usual kind of recommend. It is valid for all temple ordinances. Own-endowment patrons, or those living persons intending to be sealed for time and all eternity to a spouse, or to be married for time only, must have this regular kind of temple recommend, plus the kind referred to in category two, below.

2. ***Recommend for Living Ordinances.*** As mentioned above, this kind of a recommend is needed by those receiving their own endowment, or by those living persons being sealed for time and eternity to a

spouse, or by those being married for time only. It carries with it more statistical information than does the regular temple recommend, and thus expedites the record review process needed for those of whom this recommend is required. The recommend for living ordinances must also be accompanied by the regular temple recommend. After the recommend for living ordinances has served the purpose for which it was issued, it will no longer be needed, and the holder can rely solely on his regular temple recommend for all other purposes, until the time comes for its renewal.

3. ***Limited Use Recommend.*** This kind of recommend is issued to members from ages eight through twenty, but is good only for a limited use. That use includes baptisms for the dead, in which case the age of the participant is limited to twelve or over. It is also issued to children to be sealed to their parents, or to witness the sealing of their living brothers and sisters to their parents, or for other limited purposes.

Eligibility for Temple Ordinances

Children under eight need no recommend whatsoever to be sealed to their parents, but the family needs to present a family group record showing the relationship of the child to the family. If a person is either married or is over the age of twenty, he or she will not be issued a limited use recommend, but must be endowed, in which case he or she will be able to perform all temple ordinances, including those for which a limited use recommend is issued.

No child, of any age, can be sealed to only one parent. The sealing must always involve both parents. No woman can be in a sealed condition, in her lifetime, to more than one man.

Children born to a sealed couple are born in the covenant and need no further sealing. Children sealed to their parents by temple ordinance (including adopted children) stand in the same position as children born in the covenant. The above is clear. However, when situations arise involving the decease of one sealed spouse and the subsequent remarriage of the survivor, or the divorce of a sealed couple with children, and their subsequent remarriage, a host of difficult questions present themselves. There are applicable rules, but much room is also left for individual judgment. That judgment must ordinarily be exercised by the

First Presidency. My counsel is that when such questions arise, the temple presidency be consulted. In most cases, they will refer the matter to the First Presidency, who will exercise their inspired and sound judgment to resolve the question. I add, as a footnote, that I know of myself that these Brethren take these matters very seriously. Long are the hours they spend in prayerfully reviewing each difficult case, and, in many cases, sharing in the sorrow to which these agonizing questions give rise. I suggest that you remember these brethren in your prayers, for they need moral support in carrying out these arduous duties.

Members receiving their own endowment, or with the intent to be sealed, or not having lived in the ward consecutively for one year, must be interviewed by their bishop himself in order to receive their temple recommend (including the recommend for living ordinances). All other members may be interviewed by any member of the bishopric for the purpose of renewing their recommend. In all cases, temple recommends must be countersigned by a member of the stake presidency, preceded by an additional interview. All recommends must be renewed every year.

To receive one's endowment, one must have been a member of the Church one full year. This time-limit may be waived, but only at the discretion of the First Presidency and only for extraordinarily exceptional reasons. Limited-use recommends for baptismal purposes, however, may be issued during that one-year waiting period.

The sealing of a wife to her husband cannot be performed within less than one year following a civil marriage because the Church feels that to lessen the time interval between the two events would be to encourage couples to be married civilly and then to follow that marriage, soon thereafter, by a temple sealing. This, in turn, tends to foster the attitude that temple sealings are of lesser importance—an afterthought—inasmuch as the parties would already have become husband and wife. Those who correctly understand the importance of a temple sealing and the covenants which it entails will understand the impropriety of being married initially any other way than in the temple.

An exception involves the situation where at the time of the civil marriage one of the parties, a good member of the Church, had not been a member sufficiently long before to have become eligible for his or her endowment under the one-year rule, and therefore was ineligible to be sealed. On the date of the temple sealing, however, both parties, we will assume, were fully endowed, even though the date of the temple sealing did not meet the one-year-after-civil-marriage rule. In such a case, the postponing of the temple ceremony until after the civil ceremony is mandatory, rather than voluntary, and therefore the temple sealing is permissible. Other exceptions to this one-year-after-civil-marriage rule usually arise out of immigration difficulties, which sometimes occur in far-away places. Where an exception is desired to be made, it is suggested that clearance be obtained from the temple presidency.

It is recognized that this one-year-after-civil-marriage rule creates some heartaches for non-member mothers and fathers of faithful brides and grooms who abide by the strong recommendation that they be sealed in the temple initially. Sensitive bishops can usually use the balm of diplomacy coupled with their sweet spirit to sooth the ruffled feelings of the disappointed parents by explaining to them the marvelous blessings that will come to their children, as well as the much greater assurance that their marriage will be a successful one when sealed initially in the temple.

An exchange of rings is not part of the temple sealing ceremony, but is permitted in the sealing room immediately following the ceremony itself. It must not be performed anywhere else within the temple or on the temple grounds. An exchange of rings ceremony may occur elsewhere, as explained, but it must not in any way simulate an actual wedding or sealing ceremony and must not involve an exchange of vows. That will already have been done in the temple.

Processing Names

A few words should now be said about the procedures for handling and processing the names of ancestors which members gather for the ultimate purpose of having their temple ordinances performed. The key to understanding the present system is that responsibility for the custody of the name slips and for seeing that the work be done rests with the members themselves. This is a radical departure from previous procedures.

Let us suppose that you have gathered together the names of fifty of your ancestors. What do you do with them? First, you take them to the nearest Family History Center. There, the Temple Ready software program will clear your names, that is to say, make certain that the temple work has not already been done by somebody else for all or any one of them. It will also record the cleared names submitted by you on a diskette. Attendants at the Family History Center will be of assistance to you if you need help. The diskette will then be taken to that temple where you either intend to do the work or have it done. When the diskette arrives at the temple, it will then be processed by one of the temple's computers. The latter's printout will contain all of the names submitted, each one printed on a separate slip, one slip for each name. The slips are generally referred to as family name slips, the male slips being blue in color, and the female slips in pink. A separate ivory color is reserved for the sealing slips.

Each slip will contain the name of the ancestor in question, his date and place of birth, the name of his parents and spouse, your name and coordinates (as the one doing the submitting), plus a series of boxes for checking each of the temple ordinances to be performed, sequentially arranged, and, finally, a bar code to facilitate recording. The temple computer also prints out another sheet or sheets containing a list of all the names contained on the diskette. This sheet can be used for tracking purposes. You can come to the temple whenever you wish to personally pick up these family name slips. After that moment, you are solely responsible for their safe-keeping.

Now, the golden moment has arrived. You are ready to go to work. You have gathered together recommend holders from among your own family members, and from such friends as you have been able to recruit from your ward or elsewhere. You show up at the temple, after having alerted the temple staff ahead of time, to make certain that they are ready to receive you. If you have previously picked up your name slips, then you already have them in your possession. Otherwise, you will pick them up at the temple. You will then distribute them among your helpers and use the tracking sheet to keep track of what you have done. Then your entire group fans out and proceeds to participate in whatever ordinances you have previously agreed on. In each case, after the ordinance is performed, and before you leave the ordinance area, you will have the slip date-stamped and recorded. This makes an official record of the fact that the ordinance was done.

When the operation is over for the day, you retrieve the slips and keep them until they are used again. When all the boxes have eventually received their date-stamp on a particular name slip, the job will have been done as far as that particular person is concerned. You will have to be your own motivator to see that all your names are completely done.

The above explanation is greatly oversimplified, of course. There are many further complications involving, for example, the use of the Family Group Sheets for deceased members of your immediate family, which are handled differently. You will receive directions on how to handle them. Also, there is the matter of the availability of temple facilities, which must also be the preoccupation of the patron. For example, there is only one baptismal font, and it is not always available or properly staffed for the benefit of those who choose to present themselves at random. Advanced appointments for the use of any of the facilities is highly recommended. Smaller temples are only open at certain limited times and operate subject to certain other limitations. Some temples provide neither temple clothing nor dining facilities. What is not provided, therefore, must be brought. Before undertaking a temple excursion involving special needs, therefore, it is almost mandatory that you talk to a responsible person in the temple office, at which time the entire operation should be mapped out, making certain that the temple's facilities are ready to receive you. If you fail to do this, you risk being disappointed.

Where live sealings (whether they also involve a civil marriage or not) or one's own endowments are involved, this advance notice is important for the added reason that an entry needs to be made in advance on the temple calendar and special arrangements made. In the case of live sealings involving a civil marriage, a long lead time is even more important because the temple must conform strictly to the local and national laws governing the performance of civil marriages, and many of them require a waiting period.

Family History

In addition to attending the temple, members are encouraged to do the other things associated with family history, family record keeping, and the strengthening of the family unit. It is recommended that every member keep a journal to record important events and ideas and establish future goals. For those of advancing years, the writing of a life's history is highly recommended so that their more distant posterity may eventually know them also and love them as persons rather than as statistical abstractions. When they finally meet in the hereafter, how wonderful it will be if this meeting can be realized between loved ones, rather than between total strangers. It would be well if members started collecting all the information they can about their forebears, and placing it in a safe place. Members should interview others who have information about the family that may be unknown to the interviewers, especially where the prospective interviewee is in declining years. If this interview is delayed, it may be too late. These are lifetime projects. Let all members give them prayerful consideration, and the Lord will bless their efforts.

9

The Temple Sanctuary

God's Promised Blessings

It would be hard for even the most casual to be unimpressed by the following message from the Lord:

> And inasmuch as my people build a house unto me in the name of the Lord, and do not suffer any unclean thing to come into it, that it be not defiled, my glory shall rest upon it; yea, and my presence shall be there, for I will come into it, and all the pure in heart that shall come into it *shall see God.* But if it be defiled I will not come into it, and my glory shall not be there; for I will not come into unholy temples (D&C 97:15-16, italics added).

I have frequently pondered the meaning of those awesome verses. Were they to be taken literally, or were they mere poetic exaggeration, sometimes used to drive home an important moral principle? No doubt those verses *do* drive home a frighteningly important principle, namely, that no unholy person or thing can enter God's temple without incurring his serious displeasure. But what about the words "I will come into it, and the pure in heart . . . shall see God." Did he really mean that he was reserving his divine presence for those who could come before him in absolute purity?

I leave it up to each reader to ponder the answer to that question for himself. As for me, based upon my own experience, I believe that the Lord meant what he said.

In the chapter on protocol I explore more fully the idea that to some people, paying proper respect to holy things comes more naturally than it does to others. The Lord has given us different gifts, and, I am certain, for a wise purpose (D&C 46:11-26). But all who enter the temple, regardless of their greater or lesser propensity for showing proper respect for sacred things, must understand that when they cross the threshold of a holy temple, they enter a "house of prayer, a house of fasting, a house of faith, a house of learning, a house of glory, a house of order, a house of God" (D&C 109:8). Those are the very words used by the Prophet Joseph Smith in his dedicatory prayer for the Kirtland Temple. He insisted that the words of the prayer had been given to him by the Lord himself, so they actually became the Lord's own characterization of his Kirtland Temple, and, no doubt, of all subsequent temples.

Temple Miracles

Pursuing the matter, let me recount the following incident. One day while I was in my temple office, a note was handed to me indicating that one of the boys in the baptistry had something very important to tell me. I hurried downstairs forthwith to meet the boy in the waiting area. He was about fourteen years old He had come from out of town with a busload of his teenage companions.

I was informed that he had just performed his baptismal assignment according to regular temple procedures. He had been working from a list of names, one of which was that of his own deceased grandfather, to whom he had been very closely attached before the grandfather's death. The lad told me, with trembling voice, that when he emerged from the water, his grandfather clearly appeared, and spoke to him. The young man was completely overcome, as can be well understood. Never before in all his life had he experienced anything like it. "I know it was my granddad," he said, "because he used a little expression that he and I had thought up, just between us, and that nobody else knows about."

This wonderful experience had occurred just 30 minutes before our conversation, and the boy's hair was still wet. In telling me his story, he was tearful, and he showed considerable emotion. In response to my question whether the grandfather had expressed any particular feelings of joy or otherwise, the young man answered enthusiastically in the affirmative. In fact, his grandfather had told him to tell his wife (the boy's grandmother) that everything was "O.K." I thanked the lad, and invited him, as was our custom, to give the temple a more formal account his experience.

Back in my office, I began to think about what had happened. The "attorney" part of my make-up began to ask the less skeptical part of me a lot of questions. Was the young man really telling the truth? Was he faking it? Was he fantasizing?

After prayerfully pondering the matter, I reached the conclusion that he had been telling the truth. He seemed to me to have been just a typical all-American boy. His story was told to me so artlessly and without affectation that I found him hard to disbelieve. He obviously had not been coached nor trained in dramatics. Without such training it would have been almost impossible for him to tell me such a highly emotional story unless driven by something powerful enough to have seized total control of his emotions.

After considering everything, an inner feeling finally came over me, telling me that the lad had indeed been privy to a miracle, and I use the term unblushingly. God had certified the temple's worthiness, by sending it a miraculous blessing through the instrumentality of this young man.

I should add that during the three-year period of my presidency of the Washington Temple, I was privileged to listen to a large number of experiences not unlike this one, many involving teenagers. I selected this one to relate purely at random. In fact, as I think back over the three years of my presidency, I am impressed with the fact that almost one-third of all the remarkable incidents reported to me *did* involve teenagers. This fact, in itself, is worth pondering over. Is it that the youth have not yet become tainted with the cynicism of adulthood? Is it that the Lord is blessing us with a superior generation of young people in preparation for things to come? The reader must resolve these questions for himself.

During the period we are considering, I also recall that two sisters had each been privileged to hear choirs of angels singing anthems of heavenly music. In telling me about it, they were unable to control their emotions. In one case, this miracle occurred in the celestial room and continued for many minutes.

Several temple workers reported seeing personages in the various rooms of the temple whose presence could not be accounted for by any normal explanation. In more than one case, entire congregations of persons dressed in white made their appearance. I recount these incidents with a certain diffidence, fully understanding their sacredness and the special responsibility devolving on those who are privy to them. "And now, O all ye that have imagined up unto yourselves a god who can do no miracles, I would ask of you, have all these things passed, of which I have spoken? Has the end come yet? Behold I say unto you, Nay; and God has not ceased to be a God of miracles" (Morm. 9:15). Such incidents cause one to ponder deeply on the nature and magnitude of the blessings which God is willing to bestow in his holy temples.

Respect for Holy Places

American culture is not disposed to encourage deep respect for sacred things, but a temple of the Lord cannot function without it. It is a house of peace and refinement, and of love and forgiveness. It is there that the Lord can best reveal his wishes to his servants. It is there that he can show his greatest mercy in pouring out his blessings. I urge all temple patrons to prepare themselves spiritually before entering the temple. Instead of rushing directly there from work with your mind still cluttered with the mediocrities of daily living, I suggest first spending at least a few minutes in concentrating on the fact that you are about to enter one of the most holy sanctuaries on earth. In addition, after you have finished your ordinance work in the temple, spend an appropriate amount of time in the celestial room meditating and making yourself receptive to whatever messages the Lord may have in store for you. After all, when you finally reach the Celestial Kingdom above, you certainly won't be immediately looking for a way out.

Covenants

In the temple you make covenants with the Lord. They lie at the very heart of the endowment. It is true that after your first visit to the temple, your subsequent participations are in a representative capacity for another person. But the Lord has given you this opportunity to refresh your recollection and to renew your resolve to make these covenants operative in your own life. You will never have a more sacred moment than when you make a covenant with your Heavenly Father, in a holy temple, in which each one of you makes certain promises to perform certain things, on condition that the other party will also respect his promise to perform. But of course the Lord will always do what he promises to do. "I the Lord am bound when ye do what I say; but when ye do not what I say, ye have no promise" (D&C 82:10). Thus, your blessings of eternity depend upon your faithfulness in keeping your word, solemnly given in God's presence.

Have you ever wondered whether there is a difference between a contract and a covenant, other than that the latter is more sacred? The answer is, yes, there is a difference, and an important one. A contract is between equals, legally speaking, who are in an adversarial relationship. That means that each party is expected to try to drive the best bargain he can to favor his own interests. A covenant is with God, however, and therefore is not between equals and does not create an adversarial relationship. You are not free to try to get the best bargain you can, but only to accept or reject the conditions which God gives you. If this seems like a one-sided argument, with no one to protect your interests, just remember that because God is the other party to the agreement, he has already protected your interests and has done it far better than you could do it yourself. You can be absolutely certain that whatever God asks you to do *is for your own best interest.* How wonderful it is to have this kind of a relationship with your covenanting partner.

Temple patrons would do well to ponder the words of Elder James E. Talmage on the subject of temple covenants:

> The ordinances of the endowment embody certain obligations on the part of the individual, such as covenant and promise to observe the law of strict virtue and chastity, to be charitable, benevolent, tolerant and pure; to devote both talents and material means to the spread of truth and the uplifting of the race; to maintain devotion to the cause of truth; and to seek in every way to contribute to the great preparation that the earth may be made ready to receive her King—the Lord Jesus Christ. With the taking of each covenant and assuming of each obligation a promised blessing is pronounced, contingent upon the faithful observance of the conditions.[50]

Endowment of Power

Let it not be forgotten that when construction of the Kirtland Temple was first under consideration, the temple was associated with the idea of an endowment with power from on high. "Yea, verily I say unto you,

I gave unto you a commandment that you should build a house, in the which house I design to endow those whom I have chosen with power from on high;" (D&C 95:8). This concept is reiterated in the Doctrine and Covenants, 105:12, and then again in the majestic words of the Kirtland Temple dedicatory prayer: "And we ask thee, Holy Father, that thy servants may go forth from this house armed with thy power, and that thy name may be upon them, and thy glory be round about them, and thine angels have charge over them" (D&C 109:22).

From the very beginning the words *power* and *endowment* were closely linked, and together were associated with the word "temple." From comments made by the Prophet Joseph Smith at that time, we deduce that when he spoke of visiting the temple, he had in mind receiving spiritual power which could not be obtained anywhere else.

Today, now that the ordinance of the endowment has become formalized and has been accepted as one of the required temple ordinances (see chapter 5 on Nauvoo), we must not forget that the word still retains its original meaning (as enlarged), and that it must still be regarded as referring to a special source of spiritual power. For that reason, all of our full-time missionaries receive their endowment prior to going forth to preach the everlasting gospel to the world. Thus, going to the temple must never be considered a pure formality. As before, it remains a means of revitalizing our spiritual power and of renewing our covenants before the Lord to serve him and to love him, forever.

10
The Road to Glory

God's Miracle Production

Allow me, for a moment, to indulge in a little fantasy. You are attending your favorite opera, performed in the world's most elegant theater. The vocalists and orchestra are the world's best. The stage scenery, which required months to construct, is monumental. When the performance is over, you are in ecstasy. You find yourself wondering whether there is any other dramatic production in all the world that could equal this one.

The question, however, is quickly answered: yes, there is another production that so far surpasses this one that the latter must be relegated to insignificance by comparison. The actors in this super-production are not operatic stars at all, but faithful Latter-day Saints. It has no orchestra. Its theater is the world, and its stage scenery is millions of assembled names, thousands of individual computers, family history centers, and temples scattered throughout the land. The title to this super drama is "God's Holy Temple" and its theme is "Man's Road to Glory."

Before we see the curtain rise on this miracle production, however, we mustn't forget that our forefathers had a part in it, too. They had to first set the stage by making the world ready to receive the gospel seed. It was a long and discouraging struggle. Like the builders of the stage props for the opera, our ancestors were given no major participating role to play in the finished performance, but only one of "preparing the way." But this preparatory role was terribly important, in spite of its comparative anonymity. We, their posterity, by playing our current visible roles in this super-drama, are, in a sense, paying a debt to those who made it all possible. We are fulfilling Moroni's prophecy that "the hearts of the children shall turn to their fathers,"[51] and thus open the way for the latter to take the next step on their road to eternal glory. It is the least we can do.

Preparing for Multilateral Judgment

In the chapter on Nauvoo, mention was made that salvation, from the Latter-day Saint viewpoint, is multilateral instead of unilateral. Those terms are used in the sense that when we stand before the bar of final judgment, we do not stand alone but in the company of those who have been given to us as our responsibility. ". . . the earth will be smitten with a curse unless there is a welding link of some kind or other between the fathers and the children, upon some subject or other—and behold, what is that subject? It is the baptism for the dead. *For we without them cannot be made perfect; neither can they, without us be made perfect* (D&C 128:18, italics added).

To accomplish the audacious undertaking of performing saving ordinances for every living soul who has ever lived upon the earth, much loving effort is required, and that is exactly where our current generation fits into the picture. This is our assigned role, and it is to be played out by us in today's temples erected for that very purpose.

I have made the above somewhat whimsical comparison between man's puny artistic extravaganzas and God's awesome plan for the exaltation of the entire human race in order to put temple work in its proper perspective.

Encompassing All Mankind

This celestial drama is so great and majestic as to transcend the power of the human mind to encompass it. Consider the fact that every human being who has ever drawn the breath of life, or who will ever do so (and we are talking about at least ten billion people and probably many many more), will eventually become the beneficiary of the ordinances of exaltation performed by proxy in his or her behalf.

But who is capable of forming a clear mental image of *ten billion people?* Human faces tend to blur out after about *one hundred.* Unfortunately, according to the simple principles of human behavior, enthusiasm for accomplishing any task diminishes as the visibility and clarity of its intended target fade into obscurity. To correct this, we will have to bring our target into sharper focus and reread the words of the Prophet Joseph Smith: "Those who neglect this work, do so at the peril of their own salvation."

The brake on our enthusiasm to do temple work for this infinite number of ancestors, as pointed out, is the difficulty of stretching our mind wide enough to encompass so many people. However, this is perfectly understandable. When Moses was shown ". . . . all the children of men which are, and which were created," he "greatly marveled and wondered" (Moses 1:8), and promptly "fell unto the earth," where he remained for "many hours" (vv. 9, 10). It was just too much, even for this giant.

In light of Moses' experience, perhaps we'll have to confess that the task of mentally encompassing the entire human race is quite beyond us. But we don't have to. We can start with what we have. Our enthusiasm will grow as our minds encompass more and more people. The urgency of performing this temple work so completely dominated the thinking of the Prophet Joseph Smith during his last days on earth (1840-1844) that he almost became obsessed. Having a premonition of his death, he made a valiant effort at the end to ensure that the knowledge of these ordinances of exaltation, and the authority to perform them, and an understanding of their importance should be safely transmitted to his successors before his death. In sermon after sermon the Prophet emphasized that this work had to be done. It was not an *option* but a *mandate*.

At the present time, the number of deceased persons for whom the temple work is completed each year is about one-tenth the number of persons who represent the annual increase in the world's population. Expressed differently, if we increased our temple work tenfold, we would just barely be keeping abreast of the world's population increase, *making no allowance whatever for our backlog of names*. These figures are approximate, of course, but allowing for a large margin of error, they still trumpet a message, loud and clear, that the work remaining before us is staggering.

Get Started—"As I Can, But Not as I Would"

Listen to the voice of the Lord as revealed to the Prophet in 1842, and as recorded in D&C Section 128. This particular scripture, which we accept as revelation (see v. 2), may be considered the *prologue* to our "road to glory" drama. It was given to us just as the curtain rose. Its golden rhetoric bespeaks both the "solemnities of eternity" (D&C 43:34) and the explosive enthusiasm of the message which it conveys:

> Let the mountains shout for joy, and all ye valleys cry aloud; and all ye seas and dry lands tell the wonders of your Eternal King! And ye rivers, and brooks, and rills, flow down with gladness. Let the woods and all the trees of the fields praise the Lord; and ye solid rocks weep

> for joy! And let the sun, moon, and the morning stars sing together, and let all the sons of God shout for joy! And let the eternal creations declare his name forever and ever! And again I say, how glorious is the voice we hear from heaven, proclaiming in our ears, glory, and salvation, and honor, and immortality, and eternal life; kingdoms, principalities, and powers! (D&C 128:23)

How can any believer, if acting in good faith, hear those stirring words without being moved to tears and to action? However, to those who still hesitate to answer the above trumpet call, I commend the previously mentioned eight-word epigram of the great medieval Flemish painter Jan van Eyck, "*As I can, but not as I would.*"

This message is very clear, namely, get started! We may not be satisfied with the immediate results, but at least we will have made a beginning. Like iron filings drawn toward a magnet, our yearning for perfection will draw us inexorably forward and far beyond our present mediocrity. Eventually, this will lead to the creation of personal masterpieces of eternal worth.

And so, regarding temple work, let's admit that it is impossible for our minds to picture ten or more billion people who will benefit from our work. Let's be satisfied with picturing just a few and work from there. If we do, some marvelous experiences may be in store for us, but if we do not, we lose them, forever. May I share with you a few very precious examples?

Marvelous and Miraculous Experiences

As temple president I received numerous reports (85 in one year) of workers and patrons who had had inexpressibly marvelous and miraculous experiences while performing their duties in the temple. In one case, a woman had adopted a small girl having a physical affliction, who, tragically, had died at the age of nine. During her daughter's life, this affliction had required her to unavoidably tilt her head to one side. The poor woman was frantic with grief at the loss of her little angel, who had brought so much sunshine into her home. Shortly thereafter she was participating in the ordinance of sealing her daughter to her husband and herself. As the ordinances drew to its close, the woman distinctly saw her daughter kneeling at the altar, her body apparently perfectly restored. Just before disappearing from view, however, this adorable little apparition slightly tilted her head, somewhat coquettishly, just to assure her mother that it was really she. If this good woman had been previously immobilized by an indifference to temple work, or by the fear of making a mistake, she would have been forever denied this absolutely tender and adorable experience, which changed her relationship with her Heavenly Father forever.

One of our very faithful ordinance workers was officiating on one occasion at an endowment session. The room was dark and filled almost to capacity with regular patrons, numbering about seventy-five or eighty. Suddenly there occurred an event so extraordinarily beautiful, and accompanied by feelings so indescribably overwhelming, that he could hardly control his emotions as he related it to me. According to his story: "The walls of the room, both on the right and left side, and in back, just faded away, and what I saw before me was a mighty congregation of some two thousand persons, robed in white, seated before me, and attentively watching the proceeding. They remained so positioned for several minutes, and then gradually faded away."

Who can adequately express one's feelings on such an occasion? This good brother said that it was utterly impossible for him to do so. In fact, in all of the accounts of spiritual occurrences that came to my attention, of which there were hundreds, one theme ran through them all like a golden thread, and that theme was that, confronted by such a miraculous manifestation of the power of God, the participant sensed the total inadequacy of the human language to accurately transmit his or her feelings to others. This same thought was expressed by the Prophet Joseph Smith after receiving his sublime revelation on the three degrees of glory: "Neither is man capable to make them known, for they are only to be seen and understood by the power of the Holy Spirit, which God bestows on those who love him, and purify themselves before him" (D&C 76:116).

Another patron, while in the temple, became aware of the terribly painful reality of the crucifixion of the Savior. The following verse later read by her from the Book of Mormon, seemed to validate her temple experience: "Wherefore, we would to God . . . that all men would believe in Christ, and view his death, and suffer his cross and bear the shame of the world . . ." (Jacob 1:8).

Those words are worthy of deep meditation.

These events are related by me with some hesitation and with a prayer in my own heart that they may be accepted by the reader for what they purport to be: manifestations of God's infinite love and grace for his children and his willingness to lead them by the hand through the mists of darkness and into the fullness of his heavenly light.

In talking about these very special matters, I am influenced by the spirit of the following verse in the Doctrine and Covenants: "Make not thy gift known unto any save it be those who are of thy faith. *Trifle not with sacred things*" (D&C 6:12, italics added).

Enthusiasm for Temple Work— A Special Kind of Spirituality

The error of many, in regard to temple work, is in refusing to take seriously that which God has told us that we must take seriously. By our failure to do so, we are cutting ourselves off from bounteous blessings. Note the following:

> And inasmuch as my people build a house unto me in the name of the Lord, and do not suffer any unclean thing to come into it, that it be not defiled, my glory shall rest upon it; Yea, and my presence shall be there, for I will come into it, and *all the pure in heart that shall come into it shall see God.* (D&C 97:15-16, italics added)

Those who have access to a temple within easy driving distance from their homes, but who fail to take advantage of it, need to be spiritually illuminated by hearing the shining stories of those who are required to make heroic sacrifices, such as mortgaging their homes, or selling their businesses, in order to reach a remote temple to be endowed and sealed for time and eternity. Unfortunately, another principle of human behavior seems to come into play, here, which is that the importance to us of any goal is in direct proportion to the difficulty involved in reaching it. But the Lord expects us to rise above such petty considerations of human psychology, and to see the temple in all its splendor, whether it be located a mile or a thousand miles from our home.

Enthusiasm for temple work requires a special kind of spirituality. It is the spirituality which accepts the reality of the unseen world of spirit beings, and which also recognizes the superiority of spiritual values over material values. And what are spiritual values? One cannot precisely define them, but only give examples of what they are. The scriptures abound with them.

The woman who poured costly ointment on the Savior's feet, over the objections of Judas Iscariot who would rather have sold the ointment and delivered the proceeds to the poor, was endowed with a spirituality which eluded her more materialistically minded critics.

Mary, who chose to listen to the Savior's words of life, was endowed with a type of pure spirituality which, in her sister Martha, did not burn quite as brightly. Nicodemus's failure to grasp the full significance of the Savior's insistence on the need for being "born again" [in Greek these words actually include the meaning "born from above"] conspicuously lacked the kind of spirituality which can free itself from total reliance on demonstrable proof. Remember, Nicodemus was not a bad man. On the contrary, he did have a certain kind of spirituality, but probably not the kind that prompts men and women to undertake an ambitious program of vicarious work for the dead with no more incentive than the burning feeling within them that tells them that it is the right thing to do.

The Need to Recharge Weak Spiritual Batteries

A temple patron once confessed to me that temples were not high on his list of priorities. "I would rather be helping some poor widow fix her leaky roof," he said. How could I argue against fixing a widow's leaky roof? James tells us that this kind of service is the very heart of the Christian ethic (James 1:27). For a moment, I was speechless. But the answer seemed to come to me that he was missing something. It just might be that that widow has a need even greater than getting her roof fixed. She might be grievously depressed over the loss of her husband, or afraid to die, or losing her faith, or feeling her spiritual batteries running down.

What she might need most of all is some strong person for her to plug into, to charge up her dead spiritual batteries. If all her benefactor could give her were shingles and nails, he might fail her in her hour of greatest need. In the temple, which he put low on his list of priorities, this good Samaritan who, himself, might be suffering from failing batteries, could charge them up so that when the poor widow pleaded for help, he would have something to give her. Some people find it hard to realize that for others, assurance of eternal gospel truths is the greatest treasure that life can give them—more than money, or even more than a waterproof roof.

We must remember, however, that not every temple goer ever sees a miracle. In fact, the great majority do not—at least not the kind of miracle that seems to fall outside the natural sequence of events. It is this wonderful attribute we call "faith," in the highest and purest sense of the word, which keeps our temples humming with activity, and without which they would grind to a halt. It is what enables the one to take that mighty leap from the known into the unknown and to rely on God to ensure that he or she land safely.

The Lord Tests Our Patience

Some complain that the temple ceremony is "boring." To them I have several answers. First, the Lord obviously wants us to develop patience. The interesting account of Adam's conversation with the angel of the Lord (Moses 5:5-7) makes a point of informing us that it was only after "many" days [how many is "many?" Fifty? A hundred? A thousand?] spent in offering sacrifices in obedience to the Lord's commandment, that the angel appeared and answered his questions about why he was being required to do this. During those "many days," did he get bored? Was this seemingly irrelevant detail given us to emphasize that the Lord is first testing our patience, before giving us more?

The Temple Requires Spiritual Exertion

My second point is that temple attendance requires "spiritual exertion" (these are the Prophet Joseph Smith's own words) It is a sure antidote to boredom. As I have pointed out previously, it is not correct to say that "Every time I go to the temple I learn something new." I know some somnolent temple workers who forget more than they learn and end up knowing less about the temple than they did when they started, when the experience was still new and fresh. A better way to state the above truism is this: "When I focus on the sublime drama before me, and am spiritually hungry, I receive new light on old and familiar subjects." Such a person is not likely to get bored.

Simply put, each temple experience must be regarded as an entirely new one, filled with fresh insights and learning possibilities. In fact, the word "learning" frequently appears in temple literature, such as in the dedicatory prayer of the Kirtland Temple: "Organize yourselves; prepare every needful thing, and establish a house, even a house of prayer, a house of fasting, a house of faith, *a house of learning*. . . ." D&C 109:8, italics added)

Much can be learned about the temple (without breaking the rules of confidentiality) from scriptures, and from books, some of which have been written by Church scholars for scholars, plus others written for less scholarly, but equally inquisitive minds. I recommend them for those who have the time.

Temple Ordinances Are a Form of Worship

Perhaps the most important thing to remember about the temple ordinances is that they are a form of worship, in the broadest sense of the word. It is there that we can come without distraction and interruption and devote ourselves completely to the things of God. But this requires spiritual concentration and conditioning. Upon entering the temple, we need to leave negative thoughts at the door. An inner prayer should be offered that a worshipful attitude may be sustained throughout. Nothing but the glory of God and the role to be played in implementing his rules established for the glory and eventual exaltation of his children should be on our mind.

I can personally testify that my association with the temple has brought a new dimension to my own life. I feel its influence. I feel its mellowing. I feel myself becoming a more loving and forgiving person. I feel more empathy for others in pain. I feel more driven to bear my testimony to the truth of the temple principle, which I accept and believe with all my heart.

I also feel a greater kinship with my departed ancestors and find myself reading about their lives and getting acquainted with them, even where the temple scenario does not require it. I want to know them and love them, for someday I shall embrace them as I did my own parents.

My Anchor and My North Star

Finally, the assurance that I have been sealed for time and for all eternity to my beloved wife and my children is the great joy of my life: it is both the anchor to prevent my drifting, and the north star to keep me pointed toward my eternal goals. The knowledge that the joys of my marriage are not ephemeral but eternal, and that they will continue to reverberate in an ever increasing crescendo until both of us present ourselves, pure and worthy, with our loved ones, at the foot of God's great throne, is the most important knowledge I possess.

My final thought is that temple attendance should be a joyous experience. It is a win-win situation where everybody comes out ahead. There you can probably draw closer to the Lord and to your departed ancestors than anywhere else on earth. Other buildings in the world are bigger and more sumptuous. However, there are none where the exalting ordinances of the priesthood are administered, where the sealings for eternity performed here on earth are ratified in heaven, and where they remain in force, subject to our worthiness, forever. Come to the temple! Come with joy and thanksgiving and claim your everlasting blessings.

I close with the words of one whom I sustain as a Prophet of the Lord, President Gordon B. Hinckley:

"I hope you are using [the temple] constantly, because you will gain blessings there that you cannot gain anywhere else on the face of the whole earth. The temple stands as a monument for all to see. It stands as a statement that we as a people believe in the immortality of the human soul. Everything that occurs in that temple is of an uplifting and ennobling kind, and it speaks of life here and life beyond the grave. It speaks of the importance of the individual, as a child of God. It speaks of the importance of the family, a creation of the Almighty. It speaks of the eternity of the marriage relationship. It speaks of going on to greater glory. It is a place of light, a place of peace, a place of love where we deal with things of eternity . . ."[52]

And I add to the above the words of the Lord, to the truth of which I bear witness:

"Search diligently, pray always, and be believing, and all things shall work together for your good, if ye walk uprightly and remember the covenant wherewith ye have covenanted one with another" (D&C 90:24).

Endnotes

1. *Journal of Discourses*, 2:31.

2. *Teachings of the Prophet Joseph Smith*, p. 195.

3. JS–H 1:41

4. Our modern LDS temples are also built on elevated ground, where possible. When the Saints first arrived in the Salt Lake Valley, a valid temple ordinance was actually performed on the top of Ensign Peak.

5. For further information, the reader is referred to the splendid work of Dr. Hugh Nibley, *Temple and Cosmos*, (Deseret Book Company, Salt Lake City, Utah, 1992).

6. *Answers to Gospel Questions,* p. 245.

7. *Answers to Questions,* p. 250.

8. *Answers to Gospel Questions,* p. 256.

9. See "Cloud" *LDS Bible Dictionary,* p. 647.

10. The *LDS Bible Dictionary,* p. 627.

11. *LDS Bible Dictionary,* p. 627.

12. JS–H 1:52.

13. JS–H 1:35.

14. *LDS Bible Dictionary*, p. 666.

15. *Study Bible, New Revised Standard Version,* Harper Collins 1989, pp. 130-132.

16. *The Holy Temple,* Bookcraft, 1980, p. 94.

17. See "Temple of Herod" in the *LDS Bible Dictionary,* p. 781.

18. *Mormon Doctrine*, 2nd ed., p. 60.

19. *LDS Bible Dictionary* pp. 613, 778.

20. *History of the Church,* vol. 2, p. 428.

21. Joseph Fielding Smith, *Elijah the Prophet and His Mission,* Deseret Book Company, 1957, pp. 29-30.

22. *The Holy Temple,* p. 128.

23. *Old Testament, Student Manual, 1 Kings—Malachi,* Church Education System, 1980, p. 163.

24. Bruce R. Hafen, *The Believing Heart,* second ed., Deseret Book Company, 1990, p. 5.

25. *Symbols in Stone*. Covenant Communications Inc., 1997.

26. *Gospel Symbols*, Bookcraft, Inc., 1985, pp. 1-2.

27. *Joseph Smith's Kirtland, Eyewitness Accounts,* Deseret Book Company, 1989, pp. 107-108. (From *The Life of Levi Hancock,* p. 33.)

28. M. Mark McKieran and Roger D. Launius, *An Early Latter-day Saint History: The Book of John Whitmer,* Herald House, 1980, pp. 66-67.

29. *Mormon Doctrine,* 1979, p. 436.

30. *History of the Church,* vol. 1, p. 335.

31. School of the Prophets, October 3rd, 1883.

32. *History of the Church,* vol. 1, p. 353.

33. *The Holy Temple,* Bookcraft, 1980.

34. *Writings of Joseph Smith,* p. 418.

35. J. Christopher Conkling, *A Joseph Smith Chronology,* Deseret Book Company, 1979, p. 147.

36. *Encyclopedia of Mormonism,* vol. 3, p. 1001.

37. *History of the Church,* vol. 4, pp. 492-93.

38. *History of the Church,* vol. 5, pp. 1-2.

39. *Joseph Smith the Prophet,* Bookcraft, 1989, p. 98, vol. 1, pp. 18-19.

40. *Joseph Smith Chronology,* Deseret Book Company, 1979, p. 183.

41. *Journal o f Discourses,* vol. 15, p. 81.

42. Duane S. Crowther, *Life Everlasting,* Bookcraft, 1968; Horizon Publishers, 1997).

43. *History of the Church,* vol. 6, p. 50.

44. Bruce R. McConkie, *Mormon Doctrine,* Bookcraft, 1966, p.60.

45. *Answers to Gospel Questions,* p. 90.

46. *Answers to Gospel Questions,* pp, 87-89.

47. JS–H 1:38-39.

48. Matt. 25:21; *Let Not Your Heart be Troubled,* Bookcraft, 1991, p. 257.

49. *The Holy Temple,* Bookcraft, 1980, pp 75-79.

50. *The House of the Lord,* rev. ed. Deseret Book Co, 1976, p. 84.

51. JS–H 1:39.

52. *Ensign*, September 1997, p. 72.

Bibliography

Anderson, Karl R., *Joseph Smith's Kirtland.* Salt Lake City, Utah: Deseret Book Company, 1989.

Brown, Matthew B. and Smith, Paul Thomas, *Symbols in Stone.* American Fork, Utah: Covenant Communications, Inc., 1997.

Conkling, J. Christopher, *A Joseph Smith Chronology.* Salt Lake City, Utah: Deseret Book Company, 1979.

Crowther, Duane S., *Life Everlasting.* Bountiful, Utah: Horizon Publishers, first. rev. ed. 1997.

Endowed from on High, Temple Preparations Seminar. Published by The Church of Jesus Christ of Latter-day Saints, 1995.

Hafen, Bruce C., *The Believing Heart.* Salt Lake City, Utah: Deseret Book Company, 1990.

The Harper Collins Study Bible, New Revised Standard Version. Harper Collins, 1993.

History of the Church, published by The Church of Jesus Christ of Latter-day Saints, vols. 1, 2, 3, 4, 5.

Ludlow, Daniel (ed.), *Encyclopedia of Mormonism.* New York: Macmillan Publishing Company; Toronto, Canada: Maxwell Macmillan; New York, Oxford, England, Singapore, and Sidney, Australia: Maxwell Macmillan International, 1992, vols. 1, 2, 3, 4.

Madsen, Truman G., *Joseph Smith the Prophet.* Salt Lake City, Utah: Bookcraft, 1989.

McConkie, Bruce R., *Mormon Doctrine.* Salt Lake City, Utah: Bookcraft, Inc., 1979.

McConkie, Joseph Fielding, *Gospel Symbolism.* Salt Lake City, Utah: Bookcraft, Inc., 1985.

Nibley, Hugh, *Temple and Cosmos*. Salt Lake City, Utah: Deseret Book Company, and Provo, Utah: Foundation for Ancient Research and Mormon Studies (FARMS), 1992.

Old Testament Student Manual, Religion 302, 1 Kings–Malachi. Prepared by the Church Education System, and published by The Church of Jesus Christ of Latter-day Saints, 1982.

Packer, Boyd Boyd K., *The Holy Temple*. Salt Lake City, Utah: Bookcraft, 1980

Roberts, B. H., *A Comprehensive History of the Church, vol. 2*. Salt Lake City, Utah: Deseret News Press, 1930.

Smith, Joseph, *The Journal of Joseph*. Provo, Utah: Council Press, 1979.

Smith, Joseph Fielding, *Teachings of the Prophet Joseph Smith*. Salt Lake City, Utah: Deseret Book Company, 1977.

______, *Answers to Gospel Questions*. Published by the First Presidency of The Church of Jesus Christ of Latter-day Saints, 1972-1973.

Talmage, James E., *The House of the Lord*. Salt Lake City, Utah: Bookcraft Publishers, 1962.

In addition to the above referenced tests, I make frequent citations to all four of the Church's canonized scriptures.

Index

U

V

W

Y

Z

About the Author

David S. King was born in Salt Lake City, Utah, on June 20, 1917. His father, William H. King, was of pioneer stock, having been born in Fillmore, Utah, in 1862. He served in the United States Senate, representing the State of Utah, for twenty-four years. David's mother, Vera Sjodahl King, was the daughter of Jan Madsen Sjodahl, a Mormon scholar, and author of several books on Mormon doctrine.

Elder King graduated from the University of Utah in 1937 and then labored for two years as a missionary in the British Mission. He later graduated from the Georgetown College of Law and then commenced practicing law, first in Washington, D.C. and then in Salt Lake City.

Between the years 1944 and 1958 He practiced law in Salt Lake City. During that time, he also served on two high councils, taught LDS seminary for two years, and served in the General Superintendency of the Mutual Improvement Association for about nine years.

In 1958 He was elected to the United States House of Representatives, and served there for a total of six years. After that he was appointed United States Ambassador to the Malagasy Republic and to Mauritius, where he worked for approximately three years.

Upon his return to the United States, he served for seven-and-a-half years as Bishop of the Kensington Ward in Maryland. From 1986 through 1989 he was President of the Haiti-Port-au-Prince Mission, and from 1990 through 1993 he served as President of the Washington D.C. Temple. Shorty following that, he was ordained an LDS Patriarch, which position he still holds.

Elder King married Rosalie Lehner, who is the granddaughter of the late Dr. Franklin L. West, former Commissioner of Education for The Church of Jesus Christ of Latter-day Saints. He and his wife have eight children.